The Antiracist World Language Classroom

T0386504

How can you incorporate antiracist practices into specific subject areas? This essential book finally answers that question and offers a clear roadmap for introducing antiracism into the world language classroom.

Drawing on foundational and cutting-edge knowledge of antiracism, authors Hines-Gaither and Accilien address the following questions: *what* does antiracism look like in the world language classroom; *why* is it vital to implement antiracist practices relevant to your classroom or school; and *how* can you enact antiracist pedagogies and practices that enrich and benefit your classroom or school?

Aligned with the American Council on the Teaching of Foreign Languages standards, the book is filled with hands-on antiracist activities, strategies and lesson plans. The book covers all necessary topics, including designing antiracist units of study, teaching across proficiency levels, advocacy and collaboration in the community and how to facilitate self-reflection to become an active antiracist educator. The tools, prompts and resources in this book are essential for any world language teacher, department chair, or school leader.

Krishauna Hines-Gaither is the owner of Hines-Gaither Consulting, a firm dedicated to diversity and inclusion, and Vice President for Equity, Diversity and Justice at Mount Saint Mary's University, Los Angeles, CA.

Cécile Accilien is former Chair of the Interdisciplinary Studies Department and current Professor of African and African Diaspora Studies at Kennesaw State University, GA. She is Vice-President of the Haitian Studies Association and Co-Owner of Soley Consulting, LLC, a diversity, equity and inclusion firm.

The Antiracist World Language Classroom

Krishauna Hines-Gaither and Cécile Accilien

Routledge
Taylor & Francis Group
NEW YORK AND LONDON

Cover images: © Getty Images

First published 2023
by Routledge
605 Third Avenue, New York, NY 10158

and by Routledge
4 Park Square, Milton Park, Abingdon, Oxon, OX14 4RN

Routledge is an imprint of the Taylor & Francis Group, an informa business

Library of Congress Cataloging-in-Publication Data
A catalog record for this title has been requested

ISBN: 978-1-032-11064-6 (hbk)
ISBN: 978-1-032-06569-4 (pbk)
ISBN: 978-1-003-21826-5 (ebk)

DOI: 10.4324/9781003218265

Typeset in Palatino
by Newgen Publishing UK

Access the Support Material: www.routledge.com/9781032065694

To Giovanni Douglas Gaither & Zahir Mikah Accilien

May you continue to be curious as you understand, acknowledge and claim your place in the world as African American and Afro-Haitian American young men. May you always strive for antiracism and social justice, whenever and wherever you can.

In Memoriam:

- Alice Lee Cannady Gaither, a tireless advocate for education and justice
- Mattie Mae Evans, a bright light and a firecracker until the very end
- Roseline Massé, a generous and kind soul
- Salomon Augustin Sr., passionate about education for all
- Herman Bostick and Charles Hancock, our legends

Contents

Acknowledgments

We offer a special note of gratitude to Emily Dombrovskaya and Karen Adler of Routledge Press. It was a wonderful experience to work with you both. We appreciate your prompt feedback, patience, affirmations, edits and encouragement.

Sankofa is an African word from the Akan tribe of Ghana. The Akans believe that our understanding of the present is measured by the past. In drafting *The Antiracist World Language Classroom*, we pay homage to those who have laid the foundation for anti-racism. Although it would require a separate project to name those who have contributed to this work, we are grateful to them all.

We thank Cassandra Glynn for writing the foreword, and for her contributions to the language field; Christen Campbell for her constructive feedback on the manuscript and for being a sounding board; Richard de Meij for his work on the web companion site; Shana LeGrant for consulting with us and providing insights from a district level perspective.

Also, in the spirit of *Konbit*, a Haitian Kreyòl word that means "communal and cooperative labor," we have completed this work in collaboration with our world language colleagues. They shared their knowledge with us in a variety of ways, and we thank them for their generosity, commitment and time.

In addition to those aforementioned, others who contributed to this book include the following: Stephen Campitelli, Ignacio Carvajal Regidor, Marie Correa-Fernandes, Renata Creekmur, Anne François-Hurley, Michelle Fulwider-Westall, Jowel Laguerre, Cécile Lainé, Priscilla Layne, Nathalie Letourneau, Nodia C. Mena, Alice A. Miano, Lovia Mondésir, John Moran, Kimberly Nao, Peter Ojiambo, Adriana Ramírez, Andrea Scapolo, Julee Tate, Kristi Lentz Taylor, Carine Terras, Claudia Vallejo, Brenda A. Wawire and Jenniffer Whyte.

Various colleagues and students at our respective institutions, Guilford College and Kennesaw State University, have assisted with this project. Their names follow: Zhihong Chen, Laura Davis, Roxanne Donovan, Nichole Guillory, Barbara Lawrence, David Limburg, Luciane Rocha, Federica Santini, Alina Santos Agua Hedionda, Heather Scott, Mariam Sheriff, Griselda Thomas, Seneca Vaught and Kenneth Williamson.

We appreciate the College Language Association (CLA), the Haitian Studies Association (HSA), the American Council on the Teaching of Foreign Languages (ACTFL) Special Interest Group for Educators of African American Students (AAS SIG) and Educators for Antiracism. As scholars of color, these organizations have nurtured and supported us.

Lastly, we lean to the African philosophy of *Ubuntu,* meaning "I am because you are." We would like to thank the following people: Anne-Marie Accilien, Francis Accilien, Letroy Accilien, Philippe Accilien, Veronique Accilien, Olga Accilien-Gabriel, Odile Accilien-Sorger, Jessica Adams, Theresa Austin, Alessandra Benedicty-Kokken, Reginald Bess, Debra Boyd, Samantha Cooprider, James J. Davis, Christian Flaugh, Julian Douglas Gaither, Thomasine Alicia Gaither, Ayesha Hardison, Margaretta Hines, Apricot Irving, Bruno Jean-François, Ulrick Jean-Pierre, Tamari Jenkins, Tangela Hines Jones, Walter Jones Sr., Susan Mahaffey Keener, Trina Kirby, Barbara Lawrence, Valérie Loichot, Kacie Moore Jr., Shari Moore, Zena Moore, Anthony Morrison, Tracy Morrison, Nicholas Natchoo, Flaure Nicholson, Valérie Orlando, Nicole Reynolds, Sydney Richardson, Celka Straughn, Julee Tate, Jacqueline Temple, Salaama Wadud and Lee Wilberschied.

Our work now waters the seeds that you have planted.

In the tongues of a few…

Añay, Arigato, Asante, Danke, Gracias, Grazie, Jërëjëf, Merci, Mèsi, Sulpayki, Xièxiè nǐ.

Support Material

This book includes resources in the form of videos, planning tools, articles and more, which are available on the Routledge website. You can access these downloads by visiting www.routledge.com/9781032065694, then click on the tab that says "Support Material" and select the files. They will begin downloading to your computer.

Foreword

Around 2006, I met Dr. Krishauna Hines-Gaither in a special interest group meeting at the annual convention of the national language teacher organization, the American Council on the Teaching of Foreign Languages (ACTFL). This special interest group, the African-American Students SIG (AAS-SIG), focuses on advocacy and effective strategies for engaging African-American language learners, in particular. I was awestruck by the energy and community that was present in the room—not only because the teachers present cared about the same issues, but because many of them could understand each other's experiences as Black, Indigenous and people of color (BIPOC) language teachers. Dr. Hines-Gaither has been a leader in that community and influential in its growth and support of teachers aiming to create inclusive language learning spaces. It is also the space in which she became a valued colleague and friend.

When Dr. Hines-Gaither introduced me to Dr. Cécile Accilien and shared that they were writing this book, I was ecstatic because this book takes the work of the AAS-SIG to the next level and provides teachers an opportunity to learn from Black colleagues, while also affirming the work of BIPOC language educators who have been engaged in antiracist practices in their classrooms throughout their careers. Although racism is a complex topic to teach in the language classroom, it is an issue that impacts the lives of our students, BIPOC world language teachers and people in target cultures every day. Therefore, it is a topic that we simply cannot ignore when teaching about languages and cultures.

Drs. Hines-Gaither and Accilien underscore that antiracist teaching is so much more than a unit or lesson, and that it must embody all our actions in the classroom, including how we engage with and affirm our learners' identities. They address proficiency levels and provide pathways for language teachers to bring complex topics into even novice levels. Truthfully, it is imperative that we adopt antiracist pedagogy and transformative language teaching at novice levels to attract diverse learners to our programs and to help them to see themselves reflected in important topics that impact their own communities and target culture communities. If we wait to teach in this way until learners have reached a particular proficiency level, we have already failed them. This book from Drs. Hines-Gaither and Accilien serves to guide teachers in this important work of transforming language learning into more than just learning a language, but rather into helping our learners to adopt a critical view of the world around them and to disrupt and dismantle racism in their own schools, communities and beyond.

Cassandra Glynn, Ph.D.
Concordia College, Moorhead, MN

Preface

As post-colonial instructors and scholars, we are both passionate about languages and cultures. Between the two of us we speak five languages. We have been teaching languages in various academic settings for over two decades, both inside and outside of the formal classroom. We met in Cincinnati, Ohio about 10 years ago while working as language consultants for Educational Testing Services (ETS). We supervised the scoring of Advanced Placement (AP) exams (Krishauna for Spanish, Cécile for French).

While the language community often embraces us with open arms and feels like an extended family, it is not without critique. In between scoring, while chatting over meals, we often lamented about the lack of representation of people of African descent. We noted a dearth of diversity in terms of the content of the exams, the instructors who were scoring them and the ETS leadership. Our parallel frustrations brought us together.

Each year, ETS held a conference during the AP reading where scorers could present their scholarship. Although we presented our research separately to our respective Spanish and French audiences, we always presented on a topic related to antiracism. We continued to do the work of including antiracist and anticolonial scholarship both within and beyond our language communities.

Fast-forward a decade later following the murders of George Floyd, Breonna Taylor, Ahmaud Arbery and too many others, Routledge extended an invitation to Krishauna to write a book on antiracism in the world language classroom. Krishauna immediately contacted Cécile and invited her to collaborate on the project.

Because we are committed to the work of antiracism, this book is our way to give back to our field. Although we hold the pen, we honor the voices of our world language community. Our hope is that we can collectively make advances by sharing practical and tangible tools to create an antiracist classroom. We also want to acknowledge our colleagues, both past and present, who have consistently spoken truth to power. May they continue to raise their voices even higher.

Although ever-evolving, our understanding of antiracism in the world language classroom is based on the following ten principles:

1. Silence is the enemy of antiracism.
2. Being an antiracist is a conscious journey, and not a destination.
3. Racism systematically and generationally disenfranchises Black, Indigenous and People of Color (BIPOC).
4. BIPOC students and educators' survival in the academy is dependent upon an antiracist paradigm in which they can survive and thrive.
5. Since racism intersects with economics, class, gender, sexuality, religion, ability and other identities, White people can be similarly impacted by these systems of oppression, hence the necessity for solidarity.
6. Educators need to understand that an antiracist classroom undeniably changes the game for students of color, while also enabling White students to understand how privilege, power and positionality play out in White dominant cultures.
7. An educator who wants to create an antiracist world language classroom must build the capacity to talk about race in an ongoing manner.
8. Educators must have self-accountability and be willing to work to create an antiracist, diverse, inclusive and equitable culture in their classrooms.
9. Educators should be mindful that being social justice oriented does not automatically equate to being antiracist.
10. Educators need to acknowledge that the majority of our textbooks and curricula have thrived on racist practices that silenced the voices and omitted the experiences of people of color, and were not written by or for BIPOC scholars.

As authors, we believe it is essential to situate our positionality within the framework of *The Antiracist World Language Classroom*. We are mindful of our own positionalities, power and privilege. Antiracism calls for an ongoing self-reflective practice and self-interrogation. Ladson-Billings (1995) acknowledged, "[W]ho I am, what I believe, what experiences I have had all impact what, how, and why I research" (p. 470).

We are two Black women originally from the United States (Krishauna) and Haiti (Cécile) who have been challenged by students and colleagues to justify why we speak Spanish and French. Before even hearing her speak, some people assume that an African American cannot speak a world language fluently, and therefore have lowered expectations. Cécile has had to explain that she is from a former French colony, and she learned French in the United States where she has lived since age 11. Cécile has to justify that this is why her English and French accents are "different". These biases and microaggressions are hurtful, and make us feel undervalued in our own discipline.

For us, our teaching philosophy is grounded in the idea that teaching is learning. Therefore, we are always in the process of learning how to promote antiracism within our profession. This work is real, and this work is personal. We will not stop until we see shifting tides toward antiracism. Luckily, we are not alone.

Maya Angelou (1991) said, "I come as one, but I stand as 10,000." We are influenced by the work, philosophy and spirit of scholars and trailblazers such as Stacey Abrams, Chimamanda Adichie, Julia Alvarez, Maya Angelou, Gloria Anzaldúa, Ta-Nehisi Coates, Anna Julia Cooper, Brittney Cooper, Kimberlé Crenshaw, Edwidge Danticat, Angela Davis, Robin DiAngelo, Frantz Fanon, Anténor Fimin, Paulo Freire, Édouard Glissant, Fannie Lou Hamer, Patricia Hill Collins, bell hooks, Zora Neale Hurston, Ibram X. Kendi, Martin Luther King, Jr., Audre Lorde, Jean-Price Mars, Achille Mbembe, Toni Morrison, Assata Shakur, Sojourner Truth, Harriet Tubman, Gina Athena Ulysse, Ida B. Wells, Cornell West, Carter G. Woodson and so many others on whose shoulders we stand. Reading and learning are resistance, so we continue to learn from these thought leaders and others.

As we write this book, "42 states have introduced bills or taken other steps that would restrict teaching critical race theory or limit how teachers can discuss racism and sexism" (Schwartz, 2022, para. 4). This figure has almost doubled since 2020. Our respective states of Georgia and Krishauna's home state of North Carolina are featured prominently among these 42. The writing of this book is an act of resistance, social justice and antiracism.

Our vision and hope are that our colleagues will establish antiracist world language classrooms and professional organizations, even in the face of opposition. Our intention in writing this book is to provide an additional resource, both to those in the classroom as well as administrators and leaders who are policy makers. We believe that this work is best done in collaboration, and that is why we have invited colleagues teaching a number of different languages to share their knowledge and strategies to promote antiracism. Throughout the book we also share our voices and experiences as two Black women. We uplift the power of the South African concept of *Ubuntu*, meaning *I am because we are*. We cannot fulfill this call to antiracist action without you.

We invite our colleagues, who we love so much, to take this journey with us.

References

Angelou, M. (1991). *Our Grandmothers*. Poem Hunters. www.poemhunter.com/poem/our-grandmothers/

Ladson-Billings, G. (1995). Toward a theory of culturally relevant pedagogy. *American Educational Research Journal*, 32(3), 465–491.

Schwartz, S. (2022, March 25). Map: Where critical race theory is under attack. *Education Week*. www.edweek.org/leadership/map-where-critical-race-theory-is-under-attack/2021/06

Introduction

You can't be antiracist without first understanding and unpacking who you are (identity). Next, we can begin to understand, value, and build empathy for cultures and identities that are similar and different from our own (diversity). While we are doing this, we are also learning to identify stereotypes and racism (justice), with the goal of actually speaking up and becoming an activist (action) [Quote inspired by Teaching Tolerance Social Justice Standards.].

(Cécile Lainé, French, Toward Proficiency)

In this introduction, we acclimate our readers to *The Antiracist World Language Classroom*. We begin by offering context related to our journeys as world language educators. We then bring in our readership by delineating our call to antiracism. Next, we explain the target audience for this book, followed by a presentation of antiracist definitions. We acknowledge the polarity that is often revealed through binary constructs of race and remind educators of the importance of balance when embracing

DOI: 10.4324/9781003218265-1

antiracism. Understanding the connection between social justice and antiracism, we will demonstrate their points of convergence, and also divergence.

We ground our lessons in the American Council on the Teaching of Foreign Languages' (ACTFL's) *World Readiness Standards* (WRS) while also presenting a new framework called the *Six Dimensions of Antiracism in World Languages*. New paradigms, such as antiracism, often bring fears and concerns to both learners and educators. We address those inhibitions in this introduction and throughout the book by presenting a framework that educators can use to ground discussions of race and related topics. Furthermore, we outline and complicate the common terminology used in this book because we cannot theorize race without grounding the discussion in social construction theory and critical race theory. We conclude the introduction with an overview of each chapter.

Our Collective Journey

'Discover languages, discover the world' was the slogan for ACTFL in their 2011 language promotion campaign. These words resonated with language educators across the globe. Many of us have had truly transformative experiences as a result of the intrinsic link between languages and cultures of the world. We experienced languages through multiple lenses (history, media, traveling, study abroad, relationships, cultural products such as food, music, clothing and more). We learned automatized expressions like common greetings and salutations. These linguistic and cultural elements are often a learner's first touch with world languages. Some educators have a long legacy of traveling and being exposed to different languages; others were the first in their families to acquire a passport; many took the richness of their heritage language and incorporated new knowledge.

For many who are reading this book, you may have had such a positive experience that you could not imagine any home other than the language classroom. For others who faced a more disparate journey, you learned how to face the struggle, how to negotiate your space and ultimately how to keep pressing forward even in the face of oppression. In spite of your journey, you are the educators who went beyond the two-unit requirement. You majored in a language, that language morphed into your profession, and now you stand before dozens of language learners each day to spark the same love of languages and cultures within them. No matter where you may fall on the continuum of lived experiences, we want to provide you with tools to assist you in the creation of an antiracist world language classroom. We know that the work of antiracism will constantly evolve; therefore, we look forward to continuing this journey with you.

What Is Antiracism?

There are many related definitions of antiracism. We will intersperse a few definitions that have influenced our antiracist framework, and that speak to different spheres of this work. We appreciate Kyoko Kishimoto's definition because it focuses on pedagogy while also grounding this work in institutionalized structures. **Antiracist pedagogy** means "teach[ing] about race and racism in a way that fosters critical analytical skills, which reveal the power relations behind racism and how race has been institutionalized … to create and justify inequalities" (Kishimoto, 2016, p. 541). Another definition that we find useful focuses on **systemic racism**. Some language educators have centered most of their social justice and antiracism work on the individual and interpersonal levels. In return, this has given less attention to institutional and structural levels or what is known as systemic racism.

To that end, Ibram X. Kendi's antiracist framework centers policy. Kendi (2019) wrote, "An antiracist is one who is supporting an antiracist policy that reduces racial inequity through their actions or expressing an antiracist idea" (p. 13). Embedded in Kendi's definition is the amalgamation of ideology and practice. Antiracism is not just solely a mindset shift, but also an action-oriented approach to education.

Finally, we lean to Özlem Sensoy and Robin DiAngelo's (2017) definition of antiracism. We appreciate that they offer a complex framework that addresses the individual, the interpersonal and the systemic levels of education. They also name the role of whiteness in antiracism.

> Antiracist education recognizes racism as embedded in all aspects of society and the socialization process; no one who is born into or raised into western culture can escape being socialized to participate in racist relations. Antiracist education seeks to interrupt these relations by educating people to identify, name and challenge the norms, patterns, traditions, ideologies, structures, and institutions that keep racism in place. A key aspect of this education process is to raise the consciousness of White people about what racism is and how it works. To accomplish this we must challenge the dominant conceptualization of racism as individual acts that only some bad individuals do, rather than as a system in which we are all impacted.
>
> (Sensoy & DiAngelo, 2017, p. 142)

The Antiracist World Language Classroom incorporates these three interrelated definitions of antiracism.

For whom is *The Antiracist World Language Classroom*?

This book celebrates race and culture, combats the omission of race and addresses racism and its intersections. Language educators must be unapologetic proponents of antiracist practices and policies. According to the National Museum of African American History and Culture (n.d., para 3), "Being racist or antiracist is not about who you *are*; it is about what you *do*." We call upon you, the language educator, to put antiracism into practice.

Antiracism in education should be the goal of all who touch the language classroom: students, support staff, faculty, administrators, parents, communities, business partners, legislators and board members. Although we remain exceedingly confident and hopeful in our work, unfortunately, we must acknowledge that we will not amass all members of our profession to join this paradigm shift. While we are unyielding in our call to *all* educators, our hope is that we rally a critical mass that will serve as ambassadors for this essential work. Our students' futures depend on it. As more capacity is built amongst our constituents, we will ultimately see more shifts taking place. As more antiracist educators assume strategic roles on policy-making boards, we will achieve the goal of systemic change that extends beyond the personal and interpersonal levels. Nigerian journalist and scholar Ijeoma Oluo (2019, p. 36) wrote, "When we look at racism as a system, it becomes much larger and more complicated than it seemed before--but there is also more opportunity to address the various parts of it." Our goal is to radically shift our world language classrooms and also the profession.

Antiracism for White and BIPOC Educators

In the antiracist classroom, educators who are White and educators of color are equally called upon to do this work. Far too often antiracism falls to minoritized educators and a few White allies, or as Bettina Love (2019) refers to them, co-conspirators. Sheri Spaine Long, Executive Director of the American Association of Teachers of Spanish and Portuguese, poignantly reflected,

> I am a White female, I am a language educator and humanities professor by training. I was a child during the civil rights movement…From that time, I understood that we all have to work on not being racist every day. It is a process. The educational community has a responsibility to work on this process constantly with our students collectively and individually.
>
> (Long, 2020, p. 21)

Long's quote acknowledges her positionality, centers her experience as both an individual and also part of larger societal patterns, and calls for her to actively engage in antiracism. These are productive ways for language educators to assess how their lives and experiences have influenced who they are and the type of educators they wish to become.

Antiracism at All Proficiencies

International Baccalaureate Spanish teacher of the Semiahmoo Secondary School, Adriana Ramírez shared, "BIPOC are not at the center of the production, *at all levels*, of language materials" (personal communication, July 5, 2021). In addition to our call for all educators to embrace antiracism, antiracist education must be for all proficiencies. L. J. Randolph and Stacey Margarita Johnson (2017, p. 111) acknowledged, "A principal concern with novice (and even intermediate) language students is that they have not yet developed the necessary language proficiency to engage in critical reflection and critical discussion about social justice issues in the world language classroom." This concern is shared by educators with respect to antiracism. We agree with the conclusions of Randolph and Johnson in that we affirm that you can begin incorporating antiracism from day one at all levels, including at the novice level. For example, setting the stage at the very beginning of the class may mean showing images of people of color speaking various languages in real-world contexts. While it requires planning and intentionality, we believe that *all* educators can create an antiracist classroom where their students have the opportunity to learn about the diversity pertaining to the language they are studying.

Activity

Spanish teacher in Portland, Oregon, Michelle Nicola, asks her students to generate separate lists on large Post-it papers based on Spanish and Latin American culture. A small group of students complete a list with the following headings: writers, foods, music, films, actors, countries, history, etc. Michelle places the posters on the wall and has students walk around to view the lists. She then asks students to pay attention to what is missing. They discuss who has been left out of the lists, and what more should be included such as women, LGBTQIA, BIPOC and more. This activity can be a great starting point for antiracism at any proficiency level and across languages.

Antiracism for All Learners

Finally, the work of antiracism benefits all learners, not just minoritized students. Racism ultimately hurts White students and people of color. Our students become adults. Adults may have families of their own. Adults become professionals and members of our community and workforce. We cannot afford to shy away from offering our students an antiracist education. The stakes are too high. Lives depend on our ability to do our part in shifting racist mindsets. As social justice educator Lee Anne Bell and colleagues (2016, p. 2297–2298) have written, "Refusing to talk about powerful social realities does not make them go away, but rather allows racial illiteracy, confusion and misinformation to persist unchallenged."

On Terminology

We will highlight a few terms that will commonly appear throughout *The Antiracist World Language Classroom*. Other terms will be in boldface print and defined throughout the book. As per American Psychological Association guidelines, we will not hyphenate specific ethnicities, but we will capitalize them (African American, Asian American, Mexican American). We capitalize races and ethnicities such as Black, White and Brown. We will use BIPOC and POC interchangeably. We use African American when referring to descendants of Africans who are born in the United States with long legacies and histories in the United States. We use Black as a comprehensive term when referring to African descendants globally, or we will use their countries of origin. We will use Latinx to refer to mixed genders or gender diverse individuals of Latin American descent. We will use Latina or Latino when speaking of women or men respectively. However, in sentence structure we will use the a/o for gendered nouns, privileging the feminine, while also acknowledging the binary.

As language instructors, we are mindful of the use and importance of terminology. We acknowledge that many of the terms that we are using in the book could be considered contro-versial. Contexts can shift meanings just as interpretation can be altered based on one's power, privilege and positionality. We are conscious that people in different settings use various words and terminology to discuss antiracism, colorism, social justice and other related content. We present this terminology in order to create shared meaning and understanding.

Acknowledging that the terms are not universally agreed upon, we understand the evolutionary nature of language. In authoring this book, we had many conversations regarding the beauty, idiosyncrasies, problems and tensions regarding vocab-ulary. As educators, we invite you to problematize language as being static or fixed. Engage with yourselves and your students on the complexities, sensitivities and problematic features of language. One example is the ever-evolving conversation sur-rounding pronouns in romance languages that undermine gen-der diversity or gender nonconformity.

Although terms like Latinx and others show the shifts occur-ring in romance languages and gender constructs, the field has not reached a universal framework. Therefore, we will use the most marginalized identity first, followed by the dominant. We will use people-first language such as *people with disabilities*. We use LGBTQIA as an umbrella term for a range of sexual ori-entations. Also, we extract the terms from the acronym when referring to specific groups (gay or trans). We will typically cap-italize and use *Indigenous* or *Native* when referring to Native communities, while using *South Asian Indian* when referring to citizens or immigrants from India. There may be exceptions with respect to quotations, proper nouns, or content submitted by contributors. Where possible, we will attempt to maintain these standards. German professor Priscilla Layne of the University of North Carolina at Chapel Hill shared the following tips related to terminology.

Naming & Identity in Antiracist Pedagogy

It is important to use updated terminology preferred by individual groups.

- PoC (People of Color): Is there an equivalent to this term in the language you teach?
- In German, the English term is simply used.

How do minority groups who speak your language refer to themselves?

In Germany there are a variety of terms dependent on the group.

- Afrogerman or Black German (Afrodeutsch or Schwarze*r Deutsche*r)
- Turkish German (Türkisch Deutsch or Deutsch Türke/in)
- German Jewish (Jude(n), Jüdin, Deutsche*r jüdischen Glaubens)
- Vietnamese German (Viet-Deutsch)
- German of Nigerian descent (i.e. Deutsche*r nigerischer Abstammung)

Are there outdated terms that have recently been replaced?

- ~~Flüchtling~~ □ Geflüchtete (In German we no longer say "refugee," but "one who has fled.")
- ~~slave~~ □ Enslaved woman/man/people (Just like in English we no longer say slave, but enslaved people)

Priscilla Layne,
German, UNC

Caution on the Black-White Binary

Critical race theorist Juan F. Perea (2000) critiqued the Black-White binary. He stated, "Many scholars of race reproduce this paradigm when they write and act as though only the Black and the White race matter for purposes of discussing race and social policy" (Perea, 2020, p. 346). We acknowledge that the United States has a particularly problematic history as it relates to its treatment of Black bodies. Therefore, we do not shy away from including a Black-White paradigm. It exists, it is real and has real implications. That acknowledged, we also do not essentialize the Black experience. We affirm that many people of color and other marginalized identities have a sordid and complicated history with the United States and other governments around the world.

In a U.S. context, these communities include those affected by the Chinese Exclusion Act of 1882, the Japanese Internment Camps beginning in the 1940s, the various occupations and military interventions in Latin America and the Caribbean, Guam, Philippines, Puerto Rico, Japan and so many others. We name the United States' long legacy of gender and women's inequities. We acknowledge the **lesbian, gay, bisexual, transgender, queer/ questioning, intersex, asexual/agender** (LGBTQIA) oppression, the exclusion of people with disabilities, the terroristic framing of Muslims and the injustices related to immigration, imperialism, colonization, settler colonialism, etc. **Our aim is to incorporate a range of languages, geographic regions, racialized and intersecting experiences, beyond that of the Black-White binary.** For example, see the following lesson on skin tones.

ANTIRACIST WORLD LANGUAGE LESSON TEMPLATE	
Instructor	Krishauna Hines-Gaither and Zhihong Chen, Guilford College
Language	Mandarin
Language level (shorturl.at/bxFP8)	Novice Low, Elementary Schools
Theme (Include the key, central and/or overarching focus of the lesson or unit.)	Describing race in Mandarin
Essential Question(s) (Pose questions that may require more than one lesson, are open-ended, stimulate thought and spark curiosity, concern or inquiry.)	1. What are the various racial descriptions in China? 2. How is race described in your family or community? 3. What are important elements of your cultural heritage?
Antiracism Takeaway (Key antiracism perspective, understanding or focus)	◆ Skin tone is aligned with social class and standards of beauty and purity.
Lesson Objectives and Goals (Upon completion, students will be able to...)	◆ To be able to supplement vocabulary associated with skin tone. Such vocabulary is most often omitted from textbooks and Chinese curriculum. ◆ To understand the context in which different terms are used.

World Readiness Standards (https://tinyurl.com/bdh2ddwh) (Include one or more of the *World Readiness Standards* into the lesson or unit plan.)

◆ **Presentational Communication:** Learners present information, concepts and ideas to inform, explain, persuade and narrate on a variety of topics using appropriate media and adapting to various audiences of listeners, readers, or viewers
◆ **Cultural Comparisons:**

Learners use the language to investigate, explain and reflect on the concept of culture through comparisons of the cultures studied and their own.

ANTIRACIST WORLD LANGUAGE LESSON TEMPLATE	
Language Goal	Learn vocabulary related to skin tone.
Six Dimensions of Antiracism in World Languages (Include one or more of the *Six Dimensions of Antiracism in World Languages* into the lesson or unit plan.)	◆ **Personal/Individual:** Address how race, ethnicity, racism, antiracism and other forms of oppression operate on a personal level. ◆ **Interpersonal:** Address how race, ethnicity, racism, antiracism and other forms of oppression operate on an interpersonal level. ◆ **Cultural/Societal:** Address how race, ethnicity, racism, antiracism and other forms of oppression operate on cultural and societal levels.

Activities (Include activities, tasks and engagements that serve to reach the lesson goals, objectives and/or respond to the essential question(s).)

◆ Give students a sheet and ask them to illustrate and to color a picture of themselves.
◆ Use their drawings to discuss the beauty of race and diversity. Present "difference" as positive and affirming.
◆ Show students images of Chinese people of different shades (from different regions, mixed, of Latin descent, of African descent, etc.).
◆ Show students images of people with different skin tones from around the world. (See resources that follow.)
◆ Students will label their images with the Chinese words that depict the skin tone represented. (See the following list of skin tones.)

1. 棕色, **Brown.**
2. 古铜, **Brown skin**. It's deemed healthy and attractive.
3. 桃花, **Peach, pink or light red.** Associated often with the color of a girl's face.
4. 黑炭, **Black wood charcoal. Dark Black.** Often has a negative connotation and is viewed as unattractive. This term is often used for manual laborers who are overly tanned by the sunlight or whose skin is covered by dirt.
5. 黝黑, **Dark-skinned, swarthy, deep-tanned**: Normally associated with good health and energy, and being physically active. This term is far more common than 黑炭, the 4th term listed in the above example.
6. 混血儿, **A mixed person**. Meaning of mixed ethnic or racial backgrounds.
7. 胜雪, **More White than snow, White.** Often associated with beauty and healthy color of skin although this term is rarely used. Not common at all.
8. 白皙 or 白净, **Meaning White and clean**
9. 苍白, **Pale White.** Often associated with poor health and illness.
10. 灰暗, **Gray.** Often associated with sadness.
11. 黄, **Meaning "yellow"**. This character is often used to refer to the Chinese people or the "yellow race."

ANTIRACIST WORLD LANGUAGE LESSON TEMPLATE
12. 蜡黄, **Yellow.** This term literally means "Beeswax yellow." It is often used to refer to the face color of a person who is in poor health or in a state of shock/being frightened/depression. 13. 凝脂, **Congealed cream, creamy White**. Associated with beauty, smooth and shiny skin. The translation for 凝脂 seems to be correct. 14. 冰肌玉骨, **Mainly refers to the way one carries oneself, normally used for women.** It goes beyond the skin color. The first two characters "冰肌" mean "icy or pure flesh without any blemish" (this includes the skin); the last two characters "玉骨" literally mean "jade bones." Jade is pure, cool, upright and precious. So, altogether, "冰肌玉骨" could be roughly translated as "unblemished flesh and pure bones." It often refers to a pure, delicate, upright, unbent spirit in a person.
Modification ◆ For future lessons or for Novice Mid or Novice High, discuss the connotations of each word related to skin tone.
Assessments (Include summative or formative assessment delineated by communicative, interpretive and/or presentational modes.):   Students work with their families or communities to create a poster describing themselves.* At minimum, the poster should include the following: ◆ **Images:** Display images that represent oneself. ◆ **Language:** Use a few adjectives that you have learned in class to describe yourself. ◆ **Experiences:** What do you like to do with your family, community or within your culture? **Note:** * Culture can be defined as racial, ethnic or cultural group, but also within the context of faith, food, traditions, events, experiences, cultural products etc.

ANTIRACIST WORLD LANGUAGE LESSON TEMPLATE

Resources
Use Kaplan's social emotional poster set to show children of different backgrounds.

The University of North Carolina ships culture kits that represent many different cultures and that include cultural artifacts (https://tinyurl.com/2s39ry5k). Do you have something similar in your area? If not, create your own!

In All Things Balance

In addition to the Black-White binary, we also want to present balanced content. While it is essential to address oppression, we will also incorporate how we can celebrate the richness that culture brings to our classrooms. It is important that minoritized people's stories and lives are honored holistically. In *We Want to Do More Than Survive: Abolitionist Teaching and the Pursuit of Educational Freedom*, Love notes, "Abolitionist teaching is not sustainable without joy. Dark students have to enter the class-room knowing that their full selves are celebrated. Not just their culture, language, sexuality, or current circumstances but their entire selves, past, present, and future" (Love, 2019, p. 120–121).

The late Senegalese filmmaker Sembène Ousmane says that the filmmaker is the modern griot. A griot is an African storyteller and keeper of memories and histories. In addition to film, what other sources might be accessed to tell a more accurate story? *The Antiracist World Language Classroom* aims to strike this balance. To this end, antiracist educators must include stories of oppression and resistance, sorrow and joy, celebration and education and simplicity as well as complexity. Some celebrations may refer to the stories of resistance, faith, cultural survival through language (especially denigrated languages), music, dance, carnivals, literature, science, griots and more.

Distinctions between Social Justice and Antiracism

Most books and articles on social justice frame their content broadly. Many use social justice as a catchall term for fair and equitable treatment. For example, some sources reference Sonia Nieto's definition of social justice as "a philosophy, an approach, and actions that embody treating all people with fairness, respect, dignity, and generosity" (Nieto, 2010, p. 46). We affirm this definition and feel it is an important part of antiracism. However, while social justice is certainly akin to antiracism, it is not its equivalent. Sensoy and DiAngelo (2017) agree that race and other identities have been omitted from social justice definitions. Therefore, they prefer the term, **critical social justice** which includes "race, class, gender, sexuality, and ability. Critical social justice recognizes inequality as deeply embedded in the fabric of society (i.e., as structural), and actively seeks to change this" (p. xix). Antiracism fills some of these gaps.

Both social justice and antiracism have commonalities. They both seek fair and equitable treatment of marginalized members of society. Each calls for respect for human dignity. They push the boundaries of **hegemony**, which is dominance through force or coercion from one group over another. The purpose of hegemony is to achieve the interests of those in power. While social justice and antiracism certainly align, there are some distinctions. The following chart illustrates some of the distinguishing features between these two frameworks.

Social Justice Framework	Antiracist Framework
Focuses on fair and equitable treatment related to various social justice causes	Focuses on fair and equitable treatment related to race or ethnicity
Incorporates intersections of oppression	Incorporates race or ethnicity as they intersect with other forms of oppression
Names -isms (sexism, capitalism, imperialism, racism, environmentalism, etc.) as the core of oppression	Names -isms as well as whiteness, other dominant racial and ethnic groups and racist ideas and policies as the core of racism
Can omit race and focus on other forms of oppression	Must overtly name and focus on race or ethnicity in addition to other forms of oppression
May not interrogate whiteness, White privilege, White supremacy, or other dominant racial or ethnic groups	Must interrogate whiteness, White privilege, White supremacy, or other dominant racial or ethnic groups
May have no connection to antiracist social movements, but connected to other social movements that have historically omitted race such as LGBTQIA, environmentalism, women, etc..	Must have solidarity with antiracist social movements such as #Black Lives Matter, Decolonization, #SayHerName, Dreamers, #StopAnti-AsianHate, etc.
May not incorporate an analysis of race	Must incorporate an analysis of race at various levels: Personal, Interpersonal, Cultural, Institutional, Systemic/Structural

How Antiracism Connects to the Language Curriculum: ACTFL's *World-Readiness Standards*

The WRS offer five goals termed the 5Cs: Communication, Cultures, Connections, Comparisons and Communities. The five goal areas offer a practical standard for world language learning that extend beyond the classroom setting. The standards are applicable to all language levels and across all language proficiencies. They address linguistic competencies well, and add a robust framework for language acquisition and cultural fluency. While the WRS highlight the need for "diverse perspectives," they do not explicitly mention race, antiracism, social justice or similar terminology. In *The Language Educator*'s special edition on antiracism, the call for papers stated, "The *World-Readiness Standards for Learning Languages* and the Teaching Tolerance *Social Justice Standards* have natural connections, but we need to be intentional about teaching antiracism and de-colonizing curriculum in our classrooms" (*The Language Educator*, 2021, p. 1). The absence of overtly naming these critical frameworks places distance between them and antiracism. In order to fill this gap, we have developed the *Six Dimensions of Antiracism in World Languages.*

GOAL AREAS	STANDARDS		
COMMUNICATION Communicate effectively in more than one language in order to function in a variety of situations and for multiple purposes	Interpersonal Communication: Learners interact and negotiate meaning in spoken, signed, or written conversations to share information, reactions, feelings, and opinions.	Interpretive Communication: Learners understand, interpret, and analyze what is heard, read, or viewed on a variety of topics.	Presentational Communication: Learners present information, concepts, and ideas to inform, explain, persuade, and narrate on a variety of topics using appropriate media and adapting to various audiences of listeners, readers, or viewers.
CULTURES Interact with cultural competence and understanding	Relating Cultural Practices to Perspectives: Learners use the language to investigate, explain, and reflect on the relationship between the practices and perspectives of the cultures studied.	Relating Cultural Products to Perspectives: Learners use the language to investigate, explain, and reflect on the relationship between the products and perspectives of the cultures studied.	
CONNECTIONS Connect with other disciplines and acquire information and diverse perspectives in order to use the language to function in academic and career-related situations	Making Connections: Learners build, reinforce, and expand their knowledge of other disciplines while using the language to develop critical thinking and to solve problems creatively.	Acquiring Information and Diverse Perspectives: Learners access and evaluate information and diverse perspectives that are available through the language and its cultures.	
COMPARISONS Develop insight into the nature of language and culture in order to interact with cultural competence	Language Comparisons: Learners use the language to investigate, explain, and reflect on the nature of language through comparisons of the language studied and their own.	Cultural Comparisons: Learners use the language to investigate, explain, and reflect on the concept of culture through comparisons of the cultures studied and their own.	
COMMUNITIES Communicate and interact with cultural competence in order to participate in multilingual communities at home and around the world	School and Global Communities: Learners use the language both within and beyond the classroom to interact and collaborate in their community and the globalized world.	Lifelong Learning: Learners set goals and reflect on their progress in using languages for enjoyment, enrichment, and advancement.	

Six Dimensions of Antiracism in World Languages

To provide an antiracist framework for language classrooms, we devised the following dimensions.

1. Personal / Individual
2. Interpersonal
3. Cultural / Societal
4. Curricular / Classroom / Departmental
5. Institutional / District/State / National
6. Systemic / Structural / Historical

These dimensions are designed to work in tandem with the WRS (https://tinyurl.com/bdh2ddwh), *Social Justice Standards* (https://tinyurl.com/2p94bnnp), *Proficiency Guidelines* (https://tinyurl.com/2p8dm9nf), *Can-Do-Statements* (https://tinyurl.com/2p8by85b) and other foundational documents. While every antiracist lesson may not include the previous standards and guidelines, every antiracist lesson must include at least one dimension of antiracism.

The *Six Dimensions of Antiracism in World Languages* are designed to serve both learners and educators. Some dimensions may resonate and be more appropriate for educators while others are geared more toward the language learner. Nevertheless, a comprehensive antiracist program will find ways to incorporate all six dimensions+. A daily lesson may include one or two dimensions, a unit will likely include more.

SIX DIMENSIONS OF ANTIRACISM IN WORLD LANGUAGES
1. PERSONAL / INDIVIDUAL: Focus on personal introspection and individual growth and development
Language learners and/or educators will… ◆ address how race, ethnicity, racism, antiracism, colorism and other forms of oppression operate on a personal level ◆ explore the influence of race, ethnicity and culture on one's own personal and professional attitudes and behaviors ◆ address implicit and explicit biases, and examine how they impact your teaching and learning of world languages ◆ reflect upon one's attitudes and beliefs as they relate to people of color and White people in the world language classroom ◆ name your privileged and underprivileged identities and explore how they inform your teaching of world languages
2. INTERPERSONAL: Focus on relationships, belonging and communication with students and others

SIX DIMENSIONS OF ANTIRACISM IN WORLD LANGUAGES

Language learners and/or educators will…
- address how race, ethnicity, racism, antiracism, colorism and other forms of oppression operate on an interpersonal level
- explore how race, ethnicity and culture impact relationships, communications and collaborations within groups and across differences
- prepare for triggers, critical moments and tensions
- examine the politics of language, dialects and accents
- discuss how race intersects with other identities such as ethnicity, class, gender, sexuality, religion, environmentalism, immigration status, documentation status, disability, etc.
- affirm that all students are uniquely capable of being successful in world languages

3. CULTURAL / SOCIETAL: Focus on norms, unwritten rules and the social world

Language learners and/or educators will…
- address how race, ethnicity, racism, antiracism, colorism and other forms of oppression operate on cultural and societal levels
- examine how norms, expectations, values, unwritten rules, worldviews, culture, symbols and rituals impact target cultures and world languages
- consider how students' home communities, cultures and families intersect, support and add value to the world language classroom
- incorporate diverse populations, diverse experiences and diverse cultures of the target language
- incorporate the role that society plays in the world language classroom and community
- include current, historical and contemporary events in the world language classroom
- promote positive social change, activism, advocacy, awareness and justice

4. CURRICULAR / CLASSROOM / DEPARTMENTAL: Focus on course content, language program and curricular design

Language learners and/or educators will…
- address how race, ethnicity, racism, antiracism, colorism and other forms of oppression operate on curricular, classroom, program and departmental levels
- incorporate new approaches to teaching and learning languages using diverse critical theories and frameworks
- enact equitable language placement and assessment procedures and practices
- identify and disrupt bias, omissions and stereotyping in course content
- incorporate antiracist resources into the world language classroom
- incorporate marginalized voices such as Black, Indigenous, Asian, Latinx, people of color, women, LGBTQIA, people with disabilities etc.
- assess the hidden curriculum, master narratives and stock stories

SIX DIMENSIONS OF ANTIRACISM IN WORLD LANGUAGES

◆ present diverse perspectives, representations and counter stories / counternarratives.
◆ differentiate instruction so that it is more reflective of diverse students' lived experiences and learning styles
◆ connect the antiracist curriculum to the larger world language program, district, state and national goals
◆ connect the antiracist curriculum to local, national and global trends and topics
◆ promote diverse representation, participation and access in study abroad, study away and global engagements
◆ ensure that antiracism is both a celebration of race and an interrogation of race, racism and its legacies
◆ encourage textbooks to be more inclusive
◆ supplement course materials for greater inclusion

5. INSTITUTIONAL / DISTRICT / STATE / NATIONAL: Focus on policies, procedures and access from local to national levels

Language learners and/or educators will…

◆ address how race, ethnicity, racism, antiracism, colorism and other forms of oppression operate on institutional, district, state and national levels
◆ work with department, school, district, state and national leaders to promote a culture of antiracism, equity, diversity, inclusion, access and belonging
◆ engage with policy-making boards and committees to promote a culture of antiracism, equity, diversity, inclusion, access and belonging
◆ ensure that policies and practices align with antiracism goals and challenge or address those that do not
◆ collaborate with leaders (principals, guidance counselors, department chairs, curriculum coordinators, etc.) so that they increase their capacity as antiracist leaders
◆ develop and disseminate a collective departmental vision for antiracism
◆ connect the world language antiracist efforts to other disciplines and to institutional endeavors
◆ address the (under-) representation of race and other identities among students, staff, faculty and volunteers within world language programs at institutional, district, state and national levels
◆ collaborate locally and globally with non-profits, faith-based institutions, NGOs, other schools and civic and service organizations.

6. SYSTEMIC / STRUCTURAL / HISTORICAL: Focus on historical and systematic operations and legacies

Language learners and/or educators will…

◆ address how race, ethnicity, racism, antiracism, colorism and other forms of oppression operate on systemic, structural and historical levels
◆ examine the historical roots and contemporary manifestations of racial prejudice and discrimination

SIX DIMENSIONS OF ANTIRACISM IN WORLD LANGUAGES
◆ explore the role of history, government, geopolitics, colonialism, imperialism, settler colonialism and the like on education and systemic racism ◆ examine the history of whiteness and its legacies and/or other dominant groups of the target language / culture ◆ interrogate how race, ethnicity, racism, antiracism and other forms of oppression are included or excluded from framing documents such as initiatives, campaigns, conferences, conventions, committees and standards and guidelines ◆ explore the role of professional organizations and their role in framing the world language profession

When presenting formal lesson plans, we will use the following template (available at https://tinyurl.com/pazmk6x8). This template uses a backward design model that considers the overall goals of the lesson as its primary foundation. For more information on backward design see Chapter 4. This template incorporates both language goals and antiracism goals, as we believe both should work synergistically.

ANTIRACIST WORLD LANGUAGE LESSON TEMPLATE	
Instructor	
Language	
Language level	
Theme (Include the key, central and/or overarching focus of the lesson or unit.)	
Essential Question (s) (Pose questions that may require more than one lesson, are open-ended, stimulate thought and spark curiosity, concern or inquiry.)	
Antiracism Takeaway (Key antiracism perspective, understanding or focus)	
Lesson Objectives and Goals (Upon completion, students will be able to…)	
World Readiness Standards (Include one or more of the *World Readiness Standards* into the lesson or unit plan.)	

ANTIRACIST WORLD LANGUAGE LESSON TEMPLATE	
Six Dimensions of Antiracism in World Languages (Developed by Hines-Gaither) (Include one or more of the *Six Dimensions of Antiracism in World Languages* into the lesson or unit plan.)	
Activities (Include activities, tasks and engagements that serve to reach the lesson goals, objectives and/or respond to the essential question(s).):	
Assessments (Include summative or formative assessment delineated by communicative, interpretive and/or presentational modes.):	

Incorporating Antiracism into an Existing Curriculum

A common concern of world language educators is the time that it may take to design antiracist lessons. All new lessons will take time, regardless of the topic at hand. However, we will also demonstrate how antiracism can be incorporated into existing lessons and made applicable to collaborations with students and colleagues. Every topic that is already included in world language courses can be approached with an antiracist framework. For example, from day one in a French classroom the instructor can show students a map that illustrates that there is a large number of diverse French speakers outside of France. Additionally, more BIPOC speak French than Europeans. Visual maps or images of people can illuminate these factors. If you are teaching a unit on food, consider how other cultures have contributed to the food system and culinary experience. To that end, one might discuss the Moorish or Arab contributions to Spanish cuisine, or the Chinese communities that have long histories in many Latin American countries such as Cuba, Panama and Guatemala, or the South Asian Indian populations of Guadeloupe, Jamaica, Kenya, etc.

An educator can discuss food as resistance in terms of how food survived colonization and genocides or how minoritized communities created new fusions within existing food systems. One example is the Haitian staple *soup joumou* (pumpkin soup), a soup that is typically eaten on New Year's Day, which is also Haitian Independence Day. It is a symbol of Haitian identity and freedom, and was awarded protected cultural heritage status by UNESCO in 2021.

Educators can incorporate why some cuisines are considered fine dining, such as French cuisine, while others are marginalized such as Soul Food. All educators should consider how an antiracist lens adds value, depth and complexity to their course content. An example of a scaffolded lesson follows.

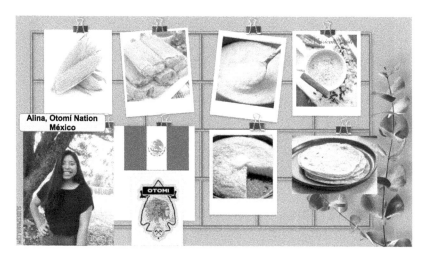

On the Web

◆ Visit this webpage Indigenous & Black Responses to Land/Food Deserts - Google Drive (https://youtu.be/cZ5uZiXBOG0) to view a video of Alina explaining the experiences of Otomí Indigenous farmers in Mexico. (Timestamp: 11:52–14:20)

At novice levels you might show students a picture of corn. Ask them what comes to mind when they think of corn. They might name some of the foods that are pictured. Present where corn is normally grown (Iowa, Illinois, Indiana, Mexico, etc.). To transition to intermediate or advanced levels, you might then discuss how corn is a staple crop of Indigenous communities in Mexico, but due to the language barrier whereby many Indigenous communities may not speak Spanish, farmers are often paid lower wages for their crops. At advanced levels you might look at land agreements to show that Indigenous groups are often disenfranchised by government policies that do not honor their land ownership rights. Another lesson could incorporate the impact of high fructose corn syrup on the human body or corn-fed animals.

Proficiency Check: Now you see how we have scaffolded a simple lesson about corn. We have gone from making a cultural connection and comparison to corn, to building on its complexity to incorporate antiracism, language bias and disenfranchisement.

What Are the Fears and Concerns Related to Antiracism?

We wish to lessen the concern that incorporating antiracism has to be time consuming. Throughout the book, we will demonstrate how antiracism can be incorporated into existing lessons while addressing common fears that may surface from students and educators when discussing race. Psychologist and racial educator, Beverly Tatum wrote in her article "Together and alone? The challenge of talking about racism on campus":

> While it is clear that intergroup dialogue can be an effective tool for building bridges and perhaps reducing what Dr. King referred to as the "fears, prejudice, pride and irrationality, which are the barriers to a truly integrated society," there are those who are understandably hesitant to participate.
>
> (2019, p. 85)

Although dominant group members and minoritized individuals may hold similar inhibitions, research (Tatum, 2019; DiAngelo, 2018; Sensoy and DiAngelo, 2017; Tochluk, 2007) shows that oftentimes their fears come from different social locations. For example, Whites or members of other dominant groups may fear the following:

◆ saying the wrong thing
◆ not having the skills or correct language to engage
◆ offending someone
◆ being vulnerable about what they do not know
◆ being automatically perceived as racist or as the oppressor

People of color or members of other minoritized groups may experience the following inhibitions:

◆ educating Whites and members of other dominant groups
◆ emotional labor
◆ retaliation (depending on power dynamics)
◆ concern that nothing will change
◆ adding yet one more task to the POC tax
◆ having to represent their entire group
◆ tokenism

We believe that incorporating the University of Michigan's model of **intergroup dialogue** (Maxwell, Nagda & Thompson, 2011) can serve as a healthy foundation for racialized discussions, and can aid in decreasing anxieties. Intergroup dialogue is defined as a roughly equal number of individuals with opposing views who come together to discuss their differences for the purpose of greater understanding. Although our classrooms may not have these equal groupings related to specific topics or identities, we can certainly use this model as a foundational framework for engaging in crucial conversations.

In *Crucial conversations: Tools for talking when stakes are high* (Patterson, Grenny, McMillan and Switzer, 2012), **crucial conversations** are defined as those that have three parts: opposing opinions, strong emotions and high stakes. The Intergroup Dialogue model can be a useful tool for framing these important discussions. The four-stage model follows. These stages will be further developed with concrete examples in Chapter 3.

Four Stages of Intergroup Dialogue

Stage 1	Group Beginnings: Forming and Building Relationships
Stage 2	Exploring the Nature of Social Identity
Stage 3	Exploring and Discussing Hot Topics
Stage 4	Action Planning and Alliance Building

THE PROGRAM ON INTERGROUP RELATIONS UNIVERSITY OF MICHIGAN

The **first stage** is community and relationship-building. We recommend that educators spend the first several weeks of school incorporating meaningful activities that will enable students to get to know their teachers and peers, and to promote self-reflection. The **second stage** is to explore social identity. For some, their social identities are very salient parts of their experience, for others, they may not have given it as much consideration. Since students will enter the classroom from very different positionalities, it is important to discuss the role that various identities have in our experiences, including, but not limited to, race, national origin, class, gender, sexuality, religion, (dis)ability, immigration and more. The **third stage** is to explore and discuss hot topics. These topics may center on social identities, current events, historical events, trending topics, social media and more. The **final stage** is action planning and alliance building. This is where students focus on how to continue to engage in the work of intergroup dialogue. The benefits of providing space for students to engage across differences are innumerable. According to Beverly Tatum,

[S]tudents have a unique opportunity to engage with people whose life experiences and viewpoints are different than their own and to develop the leadership capacity needed to function effectively in a diverse, increasingly global world. Learning to engage with others whose viewpoints are different from one's own is a citizenship skill fundamental to maintaining a healthy democracy.

(2019, pp. 80–81)

Our goal is that the language classroom will meet **language proficiency goals** as well as antiracism goals. We believe that these goals should not be exclusive, but symbiotic in that one should complement the other.

Social Construction

Italian and Portuguese professor, Giuseppe Formato (2018) noted: "Approaching pedagogy with a critical lens begins with the central notion that knowledge is socially constructed" (p. 1118). **Race** is a set of physical traits that are commonly associated with skin tone and other characteristics such as hair texture. **Ethnicity** refers to common ancestral, cultural and national experiences that distinguish one group from another. For example, a woman's ethnicity can be Latina, yet her race may be Black. We also distinguish between sex and gender. **Sex** is a biological marker of identity based on chromosomal pairings while **gender** is socially constructed and based on societal norms and codes of conduct.

What it means to be of a particular race or gender is less biological and more related to the meaning that societies have attached to certain phenotypes, physical characteristics and genders. Critical race theorists, Richard Delgado and Jean Stefancic (2017) wrote that **social construction** "holds that race and races are products of social thought and relations. Not objective, inherent, or fixed, they correspond to no biological or genetic reality; rather, races are categories that society invents, manipulates, or retires when convenient" (p. 9). We approach our work from the premise that race and racial identities are social constructs created by human beings. However, they serve to benefit some while disenfranchising others.

Activity

One way to bring the social construction of gender into the classroom is with the Gender Box Activity. You can begin with any one identity, such as *men,* and then move on to other identities such as *women, children,* etc. You can add intersecting descriptors such as White man, Black man, etc. You would repeat the same activity each time that you add a different identity. See the gender box instructions and the example that follows.

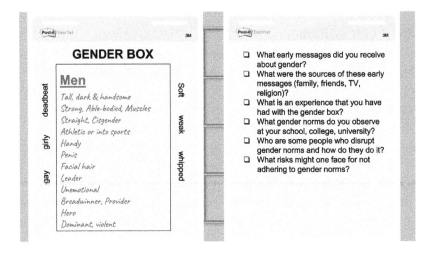

Chapter Outlines

Throughout the book we will offer practical examples of the salient points of each chapter. We draw upon the work of Paulo Freire's praxis, which is the merging of theory with practice. Each chapter will contain theory to add foundational context as well as hands-on applications. Chapters will also ask the readers to reflect and apply the content by drawing their attention to the reflective *Ask Yourself* sections. We will reference the web companion site for this book via the *On the Web* sections. We incorporate *Proficiency Checks* for most activities and lesson plans to encourage educators to include antiracism at novice proficiency levels. We will incorporate the voices of scholarly authors to provide a foundational framework for the book. Commensurately, we value the voices of world language educators. Most chapters will begin with an epigraph to center the voices of our world language community.

Chapter 1: Defining the Antiracist World Language Classroom

Chapter 1 will define antiracism and related terminology. As a theoretical framework, we will embed critical race theory, intersectionality and culturally responsive pedagogy throughout the book in a practical, accessible manner. We will articulate the need for antiracism and how it can impact world languages. We present the characteristics of an antiracist educator along with promising practices for an antiracist classroom. The chapter offers ways to set up classroom norms and guidelines. Educators will be invited to differentiate between an Antiracist Educator and a Racially Evasive Educator.

Chapter 2: Naming White Supremacy, Anti-BIPOC and Anti-Blackness

One cannot address antiracism without an interrogation of White supremacy. White supremacy is the belief or actions that indicate that White people are a superior race over Black, Indigenous and People of Color (BIPOC). This chapter will unearth the manifestations of White supremacy in world languages. The authors will explore the anti-blackness that is prevalent within many target language countries and cultures. By evaluating how White supremacy feeds anti-Black and anti-BIPOC rhetoric the chapter will serve as a foundation to incorporate other forms of marginalization. We will provide some concrete ways instructors can reshape the classroom to combat these ideologies. Finally, we present how educators can celebrate the diversities of target language communities, and also interrogate problematic practices through antiracist lessons and units.

Chapter 3: Setting the Stage for the Antiracist Classroom

Chapter 3 will focus on the antiracist world language classroom, educator and student. The first stage of antiracism begins with self. For this reason, we will call upon educators and students to examine their dispositions and proclivities as they relate to race, racism and antiracism. To this end, we present identity-based activities that focus on intersecting identities of race, class, gender, sexuality, national origin, religion and more. We share community-building activities that enable students to build relationships with their peers and openly discuss differences and similarities. We also present strategies for reframing existing curricula with an antiracist approach. These approaches will set the stage to incorporate the topic of antiracism across languages, levels and proficiencies.

Chapter 4: Designing Antiracist Units of Study

In Chapter 4, we start with the whole. Educators will create an antiracist unit of study. Using backward design, the authors will provide an outline to design an effective unit of study that centers various aspects of antiracism. The unit of study is based on content engagement across a span of time. We help educators to create an antiracist unit that allows for multiple points of engagement based on diverse content and differentiated instruction. The unit design will incorporate scaffolded ideas for novice to advanced proficiency levels, and will incorporate ideas from educators of different languages, levels and proficiencies. All units will include proficiency standards and antiracist takeaways.

Chapter 5: Planning Daily Lessons on Antiracism

Building on the skills from the previous chapter, in Chapter 5, we provide a template for planning daily lessons that focus on particular aspects of antiracism. This chapter helps educators to build antiracist lessons that range from lower risk (community building) to higher risk (antiracism) engagement. All lessons will incorporate scaffolded ideas for novice to advanced proficiency levels. Lessons include vignettes from educators of different languages, levels and proficiencies. All lessons will include proficiency standards and antiracism takeaways.

Chapter 6: Addressing Conflicts in the Antiracist Classroom

Chapter 6 will address how to set up an antiracist classroom that is equipped to manage conflict. Conflict is a normal part of any classroom environment; however, educators will likely need more preparation to address conflicts in the antiracist classroom. Educators will receive hands-on tools to lay the foundation for conflict management from the first day of class. We present strategies to manage conflict in the moment and offer approaches for how to reset after the conflict has occurred.

Chapter 7: Teaching Antiracism across Proficiency Levels

Educators often question how they can teach challenging content at different proficiency levels. The authors believe that educators should and must incorporate antiracism at all levels. Based on current proficiency standards, Chapter 7 delves deeper into proficiency. This chapter demonstrates how to teach antiracist lessons at all levels. We provide an antiracist framework for educators who teach exclusively in the target language, and also for educators who incorporate a more flexible methodology that allows for English instruction and usage. With practice and careful planning, both modes of instruction can reach the targeted learning objectives. In addition, each chapter will provide lessons, activities and/or strategies for presenting the content at multiple proficiency levels.

Chapter 8: Advocacy and Collaboration for the Antiracist World Language Classroom

This chapter will offer strategies for advocacy and collaboration among world language educators, school leaders and community members. This chapter will be essential for teachers, school and district leaders and world language professional organizations. Schools and district leaders will gain tools to work in collaboration with language educators to advocate properly on behalf of world language programs. What an individual educator may lack in antiracist preparation may be compensated by networks of solidarity which can be instrumental in filling gaps in knowledge and promoting advocacy.

References

Bell, L.A. (2016). Telling on racism: Developing a race-conscious agenda. In H.A. Neville, M.E. Gallardo and D.E. Sue (Eds),

The Myth of Racial Color Blindness (pp. 2297–2298). American Psychological Association. [Kindle locations].

Delgado, R. & Stefancic, J. (2017). *Critical Race Theory: An Introduction* (3rd ed.). New York University Press.

DiAngelo, R. (2018). *White Fragility: Why It's so Hard for White People to Talk about Racism*. Beacon Press.

Kendi, I. (2019). *How to Be an Antiracist*. Random House.

Kishimoto, K. (2016). Anti-racist pedagogy: From faculty's self-reflection to organizing within and beyond the classroom. *Race, Ethnicity and Education, 21*(4), 540–554.

Long, S.S. (2020). Race and language teaching: Sheri Spaine Long shares her personal reflections. *Language Magazine, 19*(11), 21.

Maxwell, K.E., Nagda, B., & Thompson, M. (Eds) (2011). Facilitating Intergroup Dialogues: Bridging Differences, Catalyzing Change. Stylus Publishing.

National Museum of African American History and Culture. (n.d.). Talking about race: Being antiracist… https://nmaahc.si.edu/learn/talking-about-race/topics/being-antiracist

Nieto, S. (2010). *Language, Culture, and Teaching: Critical Perspectives*. Routledge.

Patterson, K., Grenny, J., McMillan, R. and Switzer, A. (2012). *Crucial Conversations: Tools for Talking When Stakes Are High* (2nd ed.). McGraw-Hill.

Perea, J.F. (2000). The black/white binary paradigm of race. In R. Delgado, & J. Stefancic (Eds.), *Critical Race Theory: The Cutting Edge* (pp. 344–353). Temple University Press.

Randolph, L.J. & Johnson, S.M. (2017). Social justice in the language classroom: A call to action. *Dimension, 52*, 9–31.

Sensoy, O., & DiAngelo, R. (2017). *Is Everyone Really Equal? An Introduction to Key Concepts in Social Justice Education* (2nd ed.). Teachers College Press.

Tatum, B.D. (2019). Together and alone? The challenge of talking about racism on campus. *Dædalus, Journal of the American Academy of Arts and Sciences, 148*(4), 79–93.

The Language Educator. (2021, Spring). Focus topics. *16*(2), 1.

Tochluk, S. (2007). *Witnessing Whiteness:* First Steps toward an Antiracist Practice and Culture. R&L Education.

1

Defining the Antiracist World Language Classroom

For me, the fundamental elements of the Antiracist World Language Classroom are a willingness to challenge long-standing assumptions, an openness to the analysis of long-held beliefs, a willingness to accept that some of those assumptions and beliefs might be problematic, and a realization that notions of race and racism often differ from culture to culture. This is particularly important when dealing with a language such as French that is spoken around the world and serves as a vehicle for vastly different cultures.

(John Moran, French, New York University)

State Your Why!

Many educators are required to write a philosophy of teaching for their teacher education programs or for potential employers. These statements often include their positionality, essential elements of teaching and views of the learner, including diverse

DOI: 10.4324/9781003218265-2

learners. We can apply this format to the antiracist classroom. Educators should also consider their philosophy of antiracism.

First, state your positionality, who you are and how your identity impacts your practice. See our examples in the preface. Next, we encourage educators to consider why antiracism is essential to the world language classroom. What does antiracism offer to the language classroom that has been historically omitted? What gaps does antiracism fill? After delineating your personal position on antiracism, then move to the interpersonal. Reflect on how an antiracist pedagogy will impact the learners' experiences. Teachers will want to consider how an antiracist framework can be learner-centered or even learner-driven, and what laudable outcomes the educator hopes will result.

Next, consider sociologist and racial scholar Robin DiAngelo's poignant question in her Learning for Justice video titled *What's my Complicity: Talking White Fragility*. DiAngelo (2019) asked, "If you are antiracist, how would someone know?"

Ask Yourself!

◆ What evidence is there that you are an antiracist educator?
◆ What evidence is there that you are continuing to build your skills and collaborate with others?
◆ What evidence is there that you share your commitment to antiracism with others?
◆ What evidence is there that you cultivate and incorporate antiracist practices into your teaching?
◆ What evidence is there that you are open to feedback and correction on problematic aspects of your antiracist journey?
◆ What evidence is there that antiracism extends beyond your classroom to include your other colleagues and your family and community?

Antiracism and Related Initiatives

In stating your why, also consider how your antiracist framework ties into larger initiatives. While antiracism may begin on a personal level, it must be incorporated on multiple levels. See the *Six Dimensions of Antiracism in World Languages* in the introduction. To make a stronger case for antiracism, we recommend attaching your antiracism goals to other equity initiatives from local to global levels. Some examples follow.

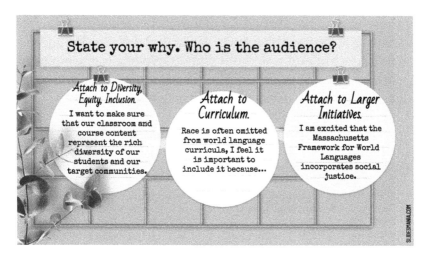

Critical Race Theory and Foundational Tenets of Antiracism

We approach the work of antiracism in the language classroom through the prism of **critical race theory** (CRT). Critical theory and pedagogy, generally speaking, seek to unearth the relationships of power inherent in education, both historically and contemporarily. Formato (2018) stated,

> Critical pedagogy identifies that all knowledge is constructed in a particular social, cultural, and historical joining of relationships. All assertions to knowledge mirror the group's particular concerns and are tied up in power relationships

(Pennycook, 1990). This argument opposes all claims that knowledge can be value-free, neutral, ahistorical, or general.
(p. 1118)

Since most world language methodologies do not incorporate antiracist frameworks, we must extend our reach to include critical theories. How might you integrate world language approaches with critical theoretical models to strengthen the antiracist classroom? We highlight language methods that informed our instruction in world languages as follows. Some of these approaches are helpful in terms of language proficiency. On the right, we have listed popular critical theories. We admonish educators to pull from both schools. No one framework will encompass all that you need. Yet, critical theory speaks to social concerns and to the dynamics of power quite prominently.

Transitioning Approaches

World Language Methods	Critical Theory
• Contextualized Language Teaching • Communicative Language Teaching • Direct (Natural Approach) • Grammar-translation • Audio-Lingual • Immersion • Total Physical Response • Task-Based Learning • Computer Assisted Language Learning • Reading Method • Suggestopedia • Community Language Learning	• Social Justice Pedagogy • Affirmative Action Pedagogy • Culturally Responsive Teaching • Feminist Theory • Queer Theory • Latinx Critical Theory • Critical Disability Studies • Critical Race Theory • Decolonization • Social construction

The Antiracist World Language Classroom is grounded in CRT and incorporates the work of Ibram X. Kendi in his book How to be an antiracist, and other noted scholars in our field. Since neither framework was created specifically for educators or world languages, we have adapted them to better serve today's educators. We center the primary tenets of CRT and antiracism, while offering ways to incorporate them into a world language classroom. A primary tenet of CRT is that racism is ordinary, systemic, personal and not exceptional. Critical antiracism educator

Ryuko Kubota (2015, p. 3) asserted: "[C]lose examinations of social structures and individual experiences will reveal that racism indeed exists in various corners of everyday life, reflecting and reinforcing racial relations of power."

Adhering to this tenet, antiracist educators must first acknowledge and admit that racism is an ordinary practice in world language classrooms. To that end, Kendi (2019, p.9) stated: "Denial is the heartbeat of racism, beating across ideologies, races, and nations." For an antiracist classroom to thrive, we must be conscious and aware of how racism shows up in the world language classroom and profession.

Another key tenet of critical race theory is **intersectionality**. Kubota (2015, p. 5) wrote: "As some scholars have noted, antiracism, as in CRT, privileges race in analyzing and critiquing social injustices, although intersectionality among race, gender, class, language, sexual identity and other social categories is emphasized by scholars of CRT" (p. 7). While *The Antiracist World Language Classroom* centers race, we do so while uplifting the multiple ways that social identities intersect. Attorney and critical race theorist Kimberlé Crenshaw is attributed with popularizing the term and providing a theoretical analysis of intersectionality. Crenshaw (1995) explained: "I used the concept of intersectionality to denote the various ways in which race and gender interact to shape the multiple dimensions of Black women's employment experiences..." (p. 358). Crenshaw's foundational work has been expanded to include the various ways that marginalized identities intersect with privileged identities. Intersectionality also demonstrates how our identities relate to power dynamics and how they manifest.

Ask Yourself!

◆ How do your identities intersect with those of your students?
◆ What do you have in common, what is distinct?
◆ How do these similarities or differences shape your engagements with your students?

To bring intersectionality to life, incorporate the Circle of Multicultural Self. This activity is inspired by the version posted by EdChange (http://edchange.org/).

Students will write their names and a hobby in the center circle. The hobby helps students to get to know their peers beyond their social identities. They will then write a few adjectives with which they strongly identify in the outer circles. Students should write a mix of identities that are presumably visible and invisible or known and unknown. Then students work in small groups to discuss the questions that follow.

IDENTITY: CIRCLE OF MULTICULTURAL SELF

Discussion Points:

1. What makes you **proud** to be a member of one of the groups that you mentioned?
2. Identify an experience where being a member of one of the groups that you mentioned caused you **pain or difficulty**.
3. What are some common **stereotype(s)** associated with 1-2 of the group memberships that you listed?
4. How do you **feel** about these stereotypes? How do you transcend them?
5. *(Share out)* Listen, share, and converse with your group members about your experiences and observations.

Teachers can modify this activity by incorporating specific identities. For example, for *education*, students might write *high school or university* in the target language. Next, have students check the box if that identity is typically *privileged or underprivileged*. Then proceed to answer the discussion questions in small groups. The modified version follows.

Activity: CIRCLE OF MULTICULTURAL SELF

Krishauna Hines-Gaither, Ph.D.
Adapted from EdChange.org

Write your name & a hobby in the center circle. Fill in the blank with adjectives that describe how you identify in each category. Check box to indicate if the position is privileged or underprivileged.

Discussion Points: First, in small groups state your name, pronouns (if comfortable) and hobby. Next, respond to one or more of the questions below.

1. What makes you proud to be a member of one of the groups that you mentioned?
2. Identify an experience where being a member of one of the groups that you mentioned caused you pain or difficulty.
3. What are some common stereotype(s) associated with 1-2 of the group memberships that you listed?
4. How do you feel about these stereotypes?
5. *(Share out)* Listen, share and converse with your group members about your experiences and observations.
6. Follow up question in large group: Ask students what they learned about their classmates that they did not know before during the Circle of Multicultural Self activity.

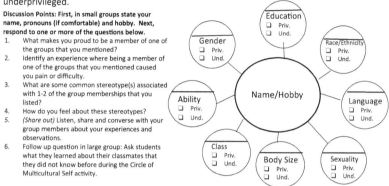

Proficiency Check: Students at novice levels should be able to complete their circles in the target language; however, the ensuing discussion may need to take place in English. The teacher can also ask each student to respond to a question in a complete sentence in the target language, and then present it to the class to bring in presentational speaking. If done in a few drafts, even at novice levels, students can give the presentation in the target language.

On the Web

◆ Visit EdChange.org to see the original version of the Circle of Multicultural Self activity.

Teachers have power in the classroom. They should use that power to help students to understand the lenses of intersectionality. This understanding creates a space where everyone can learn from one another. For example, in a Japanese language classroom the teacher can discuss the connotation and meaning behind the word *hafu*, a Japanese language term borrowed from the English word "half". *Hafu* refers to a person that has one Japanese and one non-Japanese parent. The instructor should use appropriate pedagogy in a culturally responsive manner. Pop culture could offer more context for the notion of *hafu*. See the following example which includes social media posts about the mixed-race Japanese pageant winner Ariana Miyamoto.

"That big mouth, that gaudy face. This is Miss Japan?" one person wrote on social media. Another said Miyamoto resembled an ant.

The carping was not new for Miyamoto, who attended a Japanese public school where children would refuse to touch her because "my color might rub off," she said. Fed up, she attended a U.S. high school.

> **Ariana Miyamoto**
> Miss Universe Japan, 2015.
> The first hafu woman to win
> the title.

This is an example where joy and sorrow coexist. We should be incredibly proud that Miyamoto became the first *hafu* woman to be crowned Miss Universe Japan, but also troubled by the negative racist reactions of some Japanese people.

Proficiency Check: At the novice level, ask students what are the standards of beauty in their society. The responses should be easy for novice learners to say in the target language. Some possible responses follow. Note that most of these words would appear in the first few chapters of your language textbook. What students do not know they can easily look up.

◆ Pretty
◆ Thin
◆ White
◆ Long hair
◆ Straight hair
◆ Clear skin
◆ Light skin

Ask Yourself!

◆ Why is intersectionality important in the world language classroom?

◆ What are some ways that you observe intersecting identities in your classroom?

◆ How can intersectionality be incorporated into the world language classroom?

On the Web

◆ See article Multiracial Miss Japan hopes to change mindsets. https://gulfnews.com/lifestyle/multiracial-miss-japan-hopes-to-change-mindsets-1.1484908

◆ See Kimberlé Crenshaw's TedTalk titled The urgency to talk about intersectionality. www.ted.com/talks/kimberle_crenshaw_the_urgency_of_intersectionality?language=en

Key Terminology

Continuing to unpack intersecting identities, below is some helpful terminology for the antiracist language classroom. **Racism** is any program or practice of discrimination, segregation, persecution or mistreatment based on membership in a race or ethnic group. A person who adheres to these practices would be a **racist** person. A racist act associated with the language classroom may occur when a guidance counselor does not recommend students of color for advanced language classes or outrightly discourages them from taking such classes. An **antiracist** is a person "who is actively supporting an antiracist policy that reduces racial inequity through their actions or expressing an antiracist idea" (Kendi, 2019, p. 13–25).

> **Proficiency Check:** Given the civil unrest that has been highly visible in the news of late, instructors can use signage to discuss race, even at novice levels. Students can translate signs and also create their own.

Akin to racism is oppression. Oppression refers to a situation in which people are governed in an unfair and cruel way and prevented from having opportunities and freedom. Oppression is often based on social status or social identities such as the oppression of immigrants or the oppression of Jews. Exerting power over individuals can occur at the macro level of a country's federal government agencies, policies or practices, or per the governing structure within institutions and organizations. Oppression may show up in the language program when an educator who includes lessons related to race is reprimanded because the students, parents, school or district oppose the content.

According to critical race theory, oppression is ordinary and baked into the fabric of our society and institutions. For this reason, oppression and racism can become so banal that they are difficult to recognize. One way that racism is often veiled is with the use of **aversive racism**. Aversive racism is a type of racism that functions primarily in subtle and unconscious ways. It was a term used originally to refer mainly to White liberals and educated people who have egalitarian values, but discriminatory policies and principles towards Black people and other minoritized people (*Encyclopaedia of Social Psychology*). Robin DiAngelo (2018) explained:

> Aversive racism is a manifestation of racism that well-intentioned people who see themselves as educated and progressive are more likely to exhibit. It exists under the surface of consciousness because it conflicts with consciously held beliefs of racial equality and justice. Aversive racism is a subtle but insidious form, as aversive racists enact racism in ways that allow them to maintain a positive self-image (e.g., "I have lots of friends of color"; "I judge people by the content of their character, not the color of their skin").
>
> (p. 43)

Aversive racism is prevalent in a myriad of ways in the language classroom. An example of aversive racism is when language programs have robust study abroad programs to Spain, France and Portugal, but not respectively to Latin America, the African continent or the Caribbean. When they do this, educators send a message of bias and hierarchy based on which geographic locations are noteworthy, safe, erudite and worthy of U.S. presence. This is aversive because the study abroad director never has to state that there is disdain or contempt for other geographic locations, but the actions reveal the bias. A close cousin of aversive racism is colorblind racism.

A **colorblind racist** (or the more contemporary term of color-evasive) is one who does not see color or who believes that racism is no longer the central factor determining a minority's chances (Bonilla-Silva, 2006, p. 1). For example, some educators purport, "There is no racism in Latin America, there is only classism." The denial that racism exists, and the denial that class intersects with race is a form of colorblind racism. Oluo (2019) explained: "Race as we know it in the US is closely integrated with our economic system" (p. 11). There are also intragroup dynamics whereby members of the same ethnic group may hold discriminatory views and practices based on skin tone. This intragroup bias is called colorism.

Colorism is "a powerful collection of racist policies that lead to inequities between light people and dark people, supported by racist ideas about light and dark people" (Kendi, 2019, p. 107). Due to recent skin and eye lightening, some have theorized that the baseball player Sammy Sosa is suffering from **internalized inferiority**. According to the People's Institute for Survival and Beyond (n.d., para 10), internalized inferiority is "the acceptance of and acting out of an inferior definition of self, given by the oppressor, [which] is rooted in the historical designation of one's race." Relatedly, **internalized superiority** is "the acceptance of and acting out of a superior definition [which] is rooted in the historical designation of one's race."

Activity

Ask students to gather in a circle facing one another. The purpose is to see the variety of skin tones. Look around the room at your classmates and take note of the various shades represented. If they feel comfortable sharing, students can respond to any of the following questions. Ideally a few students would respond to each question.

1. What do you love about your complexion?
2. How does your complexion compare to the rest of your family?
3. What does society say about people with your skin tone?
4. What accolades or stereotypes are associated with your skin tone?
5. Where have you observed the privilege of lighter skinned individuals over darker skinned people?
6. What comments have you received based on skin tone?
7. How has your complexion positively or negatively impacted your experiences or interaction with others?

Particularly given our context of language education and the variety of cultures represented in our discipline, we feel it is essential to address **cultural racism**. Cultural racism refers to "one who is creating a cultural standard and imposing a cultural hierarchy among racial groups" (Kendi, 2019, p. 81). This can be seen when some language educators may value and essentialize a certain form of the target language over others. For example, creating a hierarchy of Portuguese from Portugal as being better than Portuguese from Brazil. Since we engage with the politics of location as language educators, it is essential to understand the topic of geopolitics.

Activity

Spanish teacher Michelle Fulwider-Westall teaches elementary students about **attribution bias**. Attribution bias is when a person attributes a character trait to another person based upon his/her perceived race or ethnicity. Michelle does the following activity with her elementary and middle school students of the novice level.

1. Students listen to an audio clip. They do not see any images.
2. Students write or draw five characteristics that they assume about the speaker. These might include race, ethnicity, country of origin, age, gender, height, weight, etc.
3. Students discuss their five descriptions, and tell why or how they came up with those.
4. Now play the audio and watch the video.
5. Students discuss how their assumptions aligned with the visual or not.
6. In light of seeing the person speaking, students discuss their assumptions.

Geopolitics is a term invented by the Swedish political scientist Rudolf Kjellén at the turn of the twentieth century. It literally means earth or land politics. It is generally used to refer to the geography of the earth (both human and physical) and its connections to politics and international relations. In other words, what are the politics related to space and place? How does the geographical location influence one's relationship with that space? An example of geopolitics is that the vexed history between the Dominican Republic and Haiti has resulted in modern legacies of conflict and tensions that are specific to their shared island, location, space and histories. Geopolitics are often connected to colonization, race, ethnicity and ideas of inferiority/superiority. Another manifestation of superiority is whiteness.

On the Web

◆ Use the map found at https://matadornetwork.com/read/map-shows-literal-meaning-every-countrys-name/ that translates every country's name into its literal meaning to spark conversations about geopolitics and other key terminology. Click the link to see all continents.

Ask Yourself!

◆ What lessons can you create using these maps?

Whiteness is not neutral. It is a key foundation to racist policies and ideas that must be named in an antiracist classroom. Robin DiAngelo stated,

Whiteness rests upon a foundational premise: the definition of Whites as the norm or standard for human, and people of color as a deviation from that norm. Whiteness is not acknowledged by White people, and the White reference point is assumed to be universal and it is imposed on everyone. White people find it very difficult to think about whiteness as a specific state of being that could have an impact on one's life and perceptions.

(2018, p. 25)

German professor Priscilla Layne shared: "There is always a way to address the issue of race in the classroom, especially if you start by reflecting on the impact of race on your discipline" (personal communication, June 15, 2021).The limited number of resources available on antiracism in general, and antiracism in world languages in particular, highlights the lack of attention paid to this epistemology. In order to create an antiracist classroom, the educator should consciously work toward being an antiracist educator. As we seek to support our students, we have to become comfortable with naming injustice, racist policies, practices and ideas. Such naming often conflicts with our upbringing that trained us to avoid discussing race and other categories of difference, especially in mixed company.

Bettina Love (2019) stated: "In reality, many of these teachers who 'love all children' are deeply entrenched in racism, transphobia, classism, rigid ideas of gender and Islamophobia" (p. 14). Good intentions to not see color and to treat everyone the same can have negative consequences of not valuing the mélange of cultural heritage that enhances our classrooms each day. Such a position can also discourage educators from seeking the necessary tools to be culturally responsive and antiracist.

Ask Yourself!

◆ How can you address and build capacity for that which you refuse to see and acknowledge?

Kubota (2015) wrote: "Discussing racialization and racism typically arouses discomfort and a sense of threat in both everyday and academic discourses. Consequently, these topics are often tucked away in the field of language education" (p. 3). Below, we share characteristics of an antiracist educator as compared to a racially evasive educator. A racially evasive educator is one that omits race from the curriculum and avoids engaging the topics of race, ethnicity, racism, colorism or antiracism. Study the following chart of common positions taken by educators.

Characteristics of an antiracist educator versus a racially evasive educator	
Antiracist educator	*Racially evasive educator*
Outs oneself as antiracist	Makes no public declaration
Overtly names racist ideas	Does not overtly name racist ideas or uses aversive racist practices
Overtly names racist policies at institutional and systemic levels	Remains at personal and interpersonal levels
Names and sees differences	Denies or downplays differences
Sees the unique differences as assets	Sees differences as deficits or inconsequential
Displays include visible representations of diversity in a variety of ways	Displays include subject matter content that is flat and one-dimensional
Seeks positive antiracist change	Conforms to status quo, may serve as gatekeeper
Acknowledges growth gaps and weaknesses and sees them as opportunities for change	Dismisses growth gaps and weaknesses and refuses to change
Fills growth gaps through radical collaborations and knowledge seeking	Works in isolation, offers excuses for why one cannot shift to antiracist paradigms
Sees students as co-creators	Sees students as receptors
Names race, racism or antiracism	Sticks to social justice or no critical engagement at all
Interrogates the world language discipline	Sees discipline as infallible
Ever learning	Stagnate with little growth
Shifts and adapts in course content with inclusion of race, racism and antiracism	Teaches traditional lessons with little to no shift in course content
Incorporates current events and social concerns, including those seen as controversial	Shies away from current events and social concerns, especially those seen as controversial
Uses innovation, radical collaborations and creativity to combat a lack of resources	Uses lack of resources (time, money, staff) as an excuse to not engage race, racism or antiracism.

Ask Yourself!

◆ Where do you see yourself reflected (racially evasive or antiracist)?

◆ What resources do you need in order to shift from the racially evasive educator to the antiracist educator?

◆ What impact might either position have on your instruction, students or the language classroom?

Setting Community Norms

It is important to ground the class in a common classroom code for engagement. We prefer to co-construct a set of community norms or guidelines early in the course. We use norms and guidelines interchangeably. This anchoring helps to affirm the values of the learning space. Having guidelines established early also allows the students and faculty to be ready in the event that a critical moment should occur (see Chapter 6 on critical moments).

Proficiency Check: Guidelines can be constructed in English or the target language. Since some target languages can use infinitives as imperatives, this may be a good way to engage students at novice proficiency levels with little to no sentence structure needed. For logographic languages, teachers can display the character and use an image to accompany it.

Sensoy and DiAngelo (2014) caution that guidelines should benefit the marginalized, and not reinforce inequities by giving more airtime and authority to dominant voices. They stated: "This is why we have come to deny equal time to all narratives in our classrooms. Our intentions in doing so are to correct the existing power imbalances by turning down the volume on dominant narratives" (p. 3). There are several schools of thought regarding dominant voices in the classroom that align with Sensoy and DiAngelo, including affirmative action pedagogy. We lean more to the multipartial facilitator model whereby the educator states a clear position, while also encouraging diverse perspectives.

Facilitator Modalities

Impartial (Neutral)	Facilitator gives equal time to every narrative that is voiced.	1. What interests students?
Partial (Advocate)	Facilitator pushes against dominant narratives.	2. What current events or topics interest you? 3. In what are you well versed?
Multipartial (Clear position of interrogating master narratives, but invites other perspectives)	Facilitator dissects the dominant narratives to expose their limitations and encourage contributions of counter narratives.	4. What is a topic that you know less about? 5. Is every class period already planned?*

On the Web

◆ Read the article Balancing asymmetrical social power dynamics from the University of Michigan on the three facilitator models. https://drive.google.com/file/d/1EkE5hGBze7MOxahViFnYNCWv3UnwPrPQ/view

Ask Yourself!

◆ What type of facilitator are you?
◆ Might you use a certain facilitator modality in certain instances, and then incorporate others in different situations?
◆ Using the multipartial approach, how would you encourage other perspectives to join classroom discussions?

The educator will need to build the capacity of the students around social identity, which is the second stage of the Intergroup Dialogue model of the University of Michigan. As students understand the nature of social identity, they will have more of a foundation in intergroup dynamics. In typical group discussions, students may raise their hands to speak. They may simply begin speaking with no prior acknowledgment or the teacher may control the space by calling on who is next. All of these can work depending on the setting. Some strategies to bring underrepresented voices into the classroom follow:

◆ Build the capacity of students to ground their engagements in social identity theories, thus making them more conscious of intergroup dynamics, power, privilege and oppression. For example, boys often speak up first and more often. If they are aware of this, boys may be more apt to yield back the floor.
◆ Give students specific roles when working in groups to encourage multifarious participation.

◆ Use a combination of whole group and small group discussions so that students have a chance to enter the discussion at varying levels of comfort.

◆ Place a transitional object in the center of the room or in the center of the small group. When someone wishes to speak, the speaker will retrieve the object, and then have the floor. When finished, the speaker places the object back in its original position. The next speaker will retrieve the object. This structure allows students to respect the person who is speaking, take turns and practice active listening.

◆ Remind students to reflect on W.A.I.T. (Why Am I Talking? / Why Aren't I Talking?).

◆ Use the Speaker, Listener, Observer model (Egan and Price, 2018: explanation follows).

In the late 1970s, Gerard Egan, psychology professor and best-selling author of *The Skilled Helper*, established the British Triad Model to be used in counseling sessions. Kimberly Nao is an education professor at Mount Saint Mary's University-Los Angeles and a racial justice consultant. She uses the triad model—Speaker-Listener-Observer— in her classes to bring individual voices into a discussion. After first engaging in this model in a workshop, Kimberly found it useful to incorporate it into her classes when discussing matters of difference, including race.

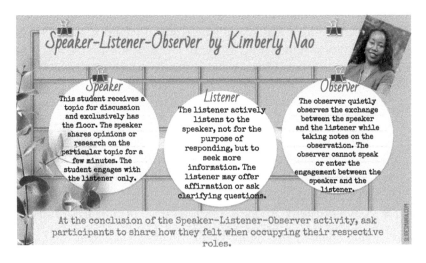

Speaker-Listener-Observer by Kimberly Nao

Speaker
This student receives a topic for discussion and exclusively has the floor. The speaker shares opinions or research on the particular topic for a few minutes. The student engages with the listener only.

Listener
The listener actively listens to the speaker, not for the purpose of responding, but to seek more information. The listener may offer affirmation or ask clarifying questions.

Observer
The observer quietly observes the exchange between the speaker and the listener while taking notes on the observation. The observer cannot speak or enter the engagement between the speaker and the listener.

At the conclusion of the Speaker-Listener-Observer activity, ask participants to share how they felt when occupying their respective roles.

Kristen A. Frey Knepp (2012) suggested engaging students in the **co-creation of a classroom code**, having them talk openly about the kind of classroom environment that would work best for them, and especially one that might work best in difficult situations or for controversial topics. Students can create the classroom norms organically as a large group exercise. For example, the teacher might ask the class, "What community guidelines, norms, or rules do we need to establish so that the classroom environment is a welcoming space for dialogues on a variety of topics, including those that may be controversial?" Educators might present some guidelines to students to initiate the conversation and then encourage them to add to the existing framework. Based on a student's previous unproductive experiences, Knepp offers the following example:

> In order to develop a class code of conduct, the professor holds a discussion with students early in the semester about uncivil behaviors they frequently see other students performing. The instructor takes notes on the discussion, then compiles a document that all students will review and sign at the next class session. By signing the code of conduct, students agree not to engage in the behaviors outlined in the document.
>
> (2012, p. 43)

Sample Guidelines for Social Justice Education Contexts

Sensoy and DiAngelo drafted the following guidelines:

◆ Strive for intellectual humility. Be willing to grapple with challenging ideas.
◆ Differentiate between opinion—which everyone has—and informed knowledge, which comes from sustained experience, study and practice. Hold your opinions lightly and with humility.
◆ Let go of personal anecdotal evidence and look at broader group-level patterns.

◆ Notice your own defensive reactions and attempt to use these reactions as entry points for gaining deeper self-knowledge, rather than as a rationale for closing off.

◆ Recognize how your own social positionality (e.g., race, class, gender, sexuality, ability) informs your perspectives and reactions to your instructor and those whose work you study in the course.

◆ Differentiate between safety and comfort. Accept discomfort as necessary for social justice growth.

◆ Identify where your learning edge is and push it. For example, whenever you think, I already know this, ask yourself, how can I take this deeper? Or, how am I applying in practice what I already know?

Krishauna Hines-Gaither often uses the following guidelines:

Community Guidelines

- **Avoid Social Justice Elitism**
  - Everyone is starting from a different foundation & location.
- **Honor first drafts:**
  - Although we may have to correct insensitivities, we acknowledge that your first statement may not be your most thoughtful response.
- **W.A.I.T.**
  - Why am I talking?
  - Why aren't I talking?

- **Lean into Discomfort**

- **Listen Actively**
  - Don't just listen to respond.
  - Be present in the space.

- **Impact vs intention**
  - Although intentions may be a "first draft" we also privilege those who may have been impacted by intentions that caused harm.

- **Others?**

Since we often lack practice in engaging in discussions about race across differences, we may not feel we have the proper preparation or we feel inhibited. Sensoy and DiAngelo recommend that educators provide students with conversation starters. These can be presented in English or the target language.

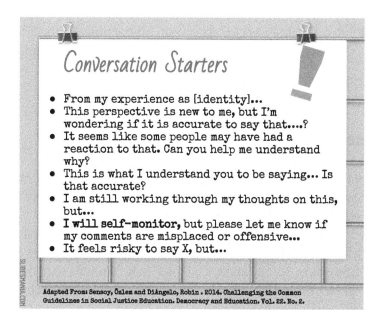

Conversation Starters

- From my experience as [identity]...
- This perspective is new to me, but I'm wondering if it is accurate to say that....?
- It seems like some people may have had a reaction to that. Can you help me understand why?
- This is what I understand you to be saying... Is that accurate?
- I am still working through my thoughts on this, but...
- I will self-monitor, but please let me know if my comments are misplaced or offensive...
- It feels risky to say X, but...

Adapted From: Sensoy, Özlem and DiAngelo, Robin. 2014. Challenging the Common Guidelines in Social Justice Education. Democracy and Education. Vol. 22. No. 2.

Ask Yourself!

◆ What guidelines do you feel are essential for a productive antiracist classroom?

◆ Will the educator generate the list first, and then ask students to add to it?

◆ Will the educator begin with a blank canvas and ask students to construct the guidelines from scratch?

On the Web

◆ Read Loretta Ross' article Speaking up without tearing down. www.learningforjustice.org/magazine/spring-2019/speaking-up-without-tearing-down

◆ Read Respect differences: Challenging common guidelines in social justice education by Sensoy and DiAngelo. https://democracyeducationjournal.org/cgi/viewcontent.cgi?article=1138&context=home

◆ Read Guidelines for classroom interactions by the University of Michigan. https://crlt.umich.edu/node/58410/printable/print

References

Bonilla-Silva, E. (2006). *Racism without racists: Color-blind racism and the persistence of racial inequality in the United States* (2nd ed.). Rowman & Littlefield Publishers.

Crenshaw, K.W. (1995). Mapping the margins: Intersectionality, identity, politics, and violence against women of color. In K. Crenshaw, N. Gotanda, G. Peller & K. Thomas (Eds.) *Critical race theory: The key writings that formed the movement* (pp. 357–383). The New Press.

DiAngelo, R. (2018). *White fragility: Why it's so hard for white people to talk about racism*. Beacon Press.

Egan, G. & Reece, R. (2018). *The skilled helper: A problem-management and opportunity-development approach to helping* (11th ed.). Cengage Learning.

Formato, G. (2018). Instilling critical pedagogy in the Italian language classroom. *Journal of Language Teaching and Research, 9*(6), 1117–1126.

Kendi, I. (2019). *How to be an antiracist*. Random House.

Knepp, K.A.F. (2012). Understanding student and faculty incivility in higher education. *The Journal of Effective Teaching, 12*(1), 32–45.

Kubota, R. (2015). Race and language learning in multicultural Canada: Towards critical antiracism. *Journal of Multilingual and Multicultural Development, 36*(1), 3–12.

Love, B.L. (2019). *We want to do more than survive: Abolitionist teaching and the pursuit of educational freedom*. Beacon Press.

Oluo, I. (2019). *So you want to talk about race*. Seal Press.

Pennycook, A. (2010). Critical and alternative directions in applied linguistics. *Australian Review of Applied Linguistics, 33*(2), 16.1–16.16.

People's Institute for Survival and Beyond. (n.d.). Our Principles. *Undoing Racism®: People's Institute for Survival and Beyond.* https://pisab.org/our-principles/

Sensoy, Ö. & DiAngelo, R. (2014). Challenging the common guidelines in social justice education. *Democracy and Education*, 22(2), 1–10.

Sensoy, Ö., & DiAngelo, R. (2017). *Is everyone really equal? An introduction to key concepts in social justice education* (2nd ed.). Teachers College Press.

Van Der Valk, A. (2019, June 11). *Teaching Tolerance Interviews Robin DiAngelo: White Fragility in the Classroom.* Video. https://youtu.be/KCxNjdewAAA

2

Naming White Supremacy, Anti-BIPOC and Anti-Blackness

As a Black teacher, any success that I had in the classroom was attributed not to my training or effort, but to the idea that students saw me as an exotic being and therefore were inclined to be "nice" to me. In reality, I have to deal with the racism of the student body as well as the institution.

(Lovia Mondésir, Haitian Kreyòl, Independent Scholar)

Early Beginnings of World Language Education

The history of language education in the United States began as an elitist offering. Watzke (2003) noted: "Classical languages (Greek and Latin) were taught as subjects for the preparation of students for entrance into higher education, often in formal tutorial or school settings" (p. 1). Given that the basis of language study has historically served as a foundation for higher education, few people had access to world languages. Some of the earliest language programs offered in the United States included Harvard University, University of North Carolina–Chapel Hill and Salem College. Many of these institutions had not yet

DOI: 10.4324/9781003218265-3

opened their doors to African Americans and other students of color. This historical context sheds light on the Eurocentric foundation of world languages, as well as the conscious or unconscious privileging of European languages.

White Supremacy

French teacher Carine Terras of the Whitfield School stated: "Education is key and ignorance is the biggest problem when it comes to racism. Opening conversations about racism and White supremacy is essential" (personal communication, August 21, 2021). What is White supremacy? How do we recognize White supremacist behaviors? Most White people do not view themselves in terms of traditional representations of White supremacy. Some of these representations have included the Ku Klux Klan, neo-Nazis, the Alt Right and more. However, White supremacy can be applied far more broadly to represent systems of superiority that serve to advantage some while disadvantaging others. The Racial Equity Tools website reported the following:

> The New York Times reports that the term "White supremacy" was used fewer than 75 times in 2010, but nearly 700 times in 2020 alone (as of the article's [shorturl.at/bfnuP] printing on October 17, 2020). In the past, the term construed extremist groups like the Ku Klux Klan and the neo-Nazis. Now this term refers to a political and socio-economic system where White people enjoy structural advantages and rights that other racial and ethnic groups do not. Many White people are unaware that this system exists, which is one of its successes.
>
> (Racial Equity Tools, n.d., para. 1)

In the context of the world language classroom, ideas related to White superiority surface in a myriad of ways. David Roediger, scholar of whiteness studies, noted: "The critical examination of whiteness, academic and not, simply involves the effort to break through the illusion that whiteness is natural, biological, normal, and not crying out for explanation" (Sandronsky, 2005). Whiteness can be so insidious that we accept it as normal and therefore it goes unchallenged. Unchallenged and unacknowledged systems of oppression cannot be combatted. Kendi (2019) stated:

> Some White people do not identify as White for the same reason they identify as not-racist: to avoid reckoning with that Whiteness—even as a construction or mirage—has informed their notions of America and identity and offered them privilege, the primary one being the privilege of being inherently normal, standard, and legal. It is a racial crime to be yourself if you are not White in America. It is a racial crime to look like yourself or empower yourself if you are not White.
>
> (p. 38)

Ask Yourself!

◆ How might you decriminalize the classroom so that it is no longer a crime to be oneself?

◆ What are some of the ways in which White supremacy is manifested in the world language profession today?

The language classroom has the opportunity to promote **radical inclusion**. This is inclusion that is not tokenizing, surface level, or relegated to one celebratory month. Instead, radical inclusion acknowledges historical and contemporary inequities, seeks to combat them and uses an antiracist framework to do so. Part of the acknowledgement process is to name the ways that White Supremacy lives in the language classroom.

Manifestations of White Supremacy in World Languages

As demonstrated in the early beginnings section above, historically language programs were exclusive spaces that were not open to all learners. Today, White supremacy is still prevalent in world language spaces. For example, language educators of color continue to be underrepresented in our field (see National Center for Education Statistics data below). Most world language professional organizations have boards that are almost all White, with little representation of people of color, and even less representation of Black people or African Americans.

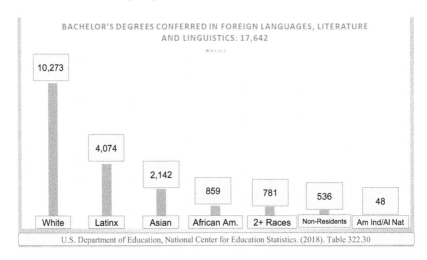

BACHELOR'S DEGREES CONFERRED IN FOREIGN LANGUAGES, LITERATURE AND LINGUISTICS: 17,642

White	Latinx	Asian	African Am.	2+ Races	Non-Residents	Am Ind/AI Nat
10,273	4,074	2,142	859	781	536	48

U.S. Department of Education, National Center for Education Statistics. (2018). Table 322.30

NCES uses the term non-resident alien, we have chosen to drop the world alien. Per NCES non-residents are defined as a person who is not a citizen or national of the United States and who is in this country on a visa or temporary basis and does not have the right to remain indefinitely. "The lack of history of slavery and colonization in these textbooks is a manifestation of the erasure of important facts that could have benefited the students." Anne Francois-Hurley, French, Arcadia University

Textbooks omit the voices of BIPOC or give them superficial treatment, leaving our teachers with limited resources. Higher level language classes have low representation of minoritized students. It is valuable for students to see themselves represented. It is beneficial for White students to have a BIPOC teacher because it may help them to receive unique perspectives of those impacted by racism, which in turn may enable them to address issues of race and bias. African American poet and educator Nikki Giovanni also states that it is important for

White students to have BIPOC educators so that they engage with people of color who are also in positions of power and authority.

Ask Yourself!

◆ How many world language teachers have you had in total?
◆ How many BIPOC language teachers have you had?
◆ If you have had a BIPOC language teacher, what was your experience?
◆ If you have not, what may have been lost by not having this experience?

Many teachers wait until students reach advanced levels to incorporate antiracism or social justice. This practice breeds inequity given that most students in general, and an even larger number of students of color, do not persist to advanced language levels. In turn, this practice omits the majority of our students from ever experiencing an antiracist world language classroom.

Although many teacher education programs incorporate disposition and diverse learners, few incorporate social justice and even fewer make mention of antiracism. The aforementioned are the types of introspections needed in an antiracist world language community. White supremacist ideas are directly connected to colonialism and imperialism, and we cannot discuss White supremacy without taking these factors into account.

Ask Yourself!

◆ While we have referenced many of the tangibles, what about the less obvious manifestations of White supremacy?
◆ Who are considered the best students in your world language program and why?

- ◆ Whose communities are represented in the classroom and school culture?
- ◆ Who speaks first, last or who is most often called upon, or not at all?
- ◆ For whom are strong letters of recommendation written?
- ◆ Who represents student leadership in language clubs and other leadership roles?
- ◆ Who is invited to present or facilitate with teachers or publish with them?
- ◆ Who is mentored by you and from whom do you receive mentorship?
- ◆ Who is consulted *before* decisions are made?
- ◆ Who is informed *after* decisions are made?

Colonialism versus Imperialism

There are many different forms of colonization such as internal and external. History and government expert Robert Longley defines **colonialism** as "an act of political and economic domination involving the control of a country and its people by settlers from a foreign power" (Longley, 2021, para 1). While colonialism is the action, the political thought or ideology that undergirds colonialism is referred to as **imperialism**. For example, the United States colonized (the act) in the name of manifest destiny (the political ideology). Manifest destiny, which was coined in 1845, is the notion that United States settlers are justifiably destined—by God, its proponents believed—to expand its control and promote democracy and capitalism across the continent of North America. **Colonization** is the act of establishing a colony. For example, Queen Isabel of Spain supported the **colonization** of Latin America via the establishment of many colonies throughout Central and South America, the Caribbean and Mexico.

The **imperialistic** foundations driving her support were economic gains as well as the idea of *civilization* to justify the pillage of Indigenous peoples in the Americas. Labeling them as *uncivilized* people made it justifiable, and using evangelism was a way to condone the crimes against the Native population. From the 15th to the 20th centuries, European colonizers used the notion of *civilization* to justify their colonial exploitation. The British and German also used that ideology.

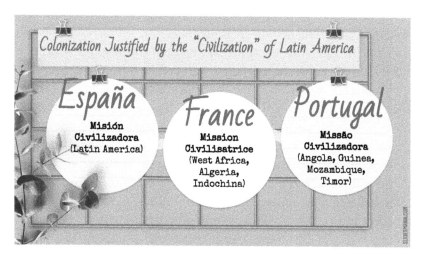

In response to civilization missions and other related histories, a Spanish teacher in the Somerville school district in Massachusetts had her students read the writings of Christopher Columbus. Finding many of his writings and practices to be atrocious, the students opted to launch a campaign. They wrote letters to the district demanding they stop celebrating Columbus Day. Though the teacher does not believe the letters were the direct rationale, later the district ceased to celebrate or recognize the holiday.

Ask Yourself!

◆ How can your classroom influence positive change?

Settler Colonialism

Indigenous scholars Tuck and Yang defined **settler colonialism** as different from other forms of colonialism in that settlers come with the intention of making a new home on the land, a homemaking that insists on settler sovereignty over all things in their new domain. Illuminating the importance of including land domination and other forms of settler domination in the antiracist classroom, Tuck and Yang (2012) stated: "We advocate for the analysis of settler colonialism within education and education research, and we position the work of Indigenous thinkers as central in unlocking the confounding aspects of public schooling" (p. 3).

Tuck and Yang also warn that colonialism is not a metaphor. This means that educators who use this term metaphorically, such as *decolonizing the curriculum*, should always tie the discourse back to the original meaning. The origins are embedded in land disenfranchisement, lest we forget. To this end, Kubota (2015) admonished, "…Canada is a settler colony which originally belonged to aboriginal people. This is an important point that any antiracist researchers and practitioners need to bear in mind…" (p. 5). Educators can incorporate the poem "Caña" by Afro-Cuban poet Nicolás Guillén (1931), whereby he problematizes settler colonialism in the context of slavery.

Proficiency Check: This poem is short, and the language is accessible for novice proficiency levels. The poem also provides a good foundation to discuss prepositions. For educators of other languages, translate this short poem, or have your students translate it into your target language.

Caña	Sugar Cane
El negro Junto al cañaveral.	The black man together with the plantation.
El yanqui Sobre el cañaveral.	The Yankee On (or above) the plantation.
La tierra Bajo el cañaveral.	The earth beneath the plantation.
¡Sangre Que se nos va!	Our blood drains out of us!

Discussion Questions

1. How does settler colonialism appear in this poem?
2. How are the different groups positioned? Why does Guillén choose the prepositions of *junto*, *sobre* and *bajo*?
3. What is the relationship between the land and the inhabitants?
4. Although Indigenous people are not named, how do their stories fold into the narrative presented in "Caña"?
5. What preposition would you align with Indigenous groups?
6. What are the enduring legacies today stemming from colonialism and domination of the past?

Ignacio Carvajal Regidor, professor of Maya K'iche' and other Indigenous languages at the University of Kansas, stated that White supremacy is manifested when some feel "entitled to access the languages of those who have been marginalized or displaced, or whose languages and language practices have been historically belittled" (personal communication, August 9, 2021).

Activity

One exercise towards naming White supremacy is to research on whose land your institution sits. For example, an instructor in Georgia can conduct research about their history of and with the Cherokee nation. Likewise, an instructor teaching French can discuss the First Nations (such as the Abenaki, Algonquin, Cree and Naskapi) that occupy the current territory known as Québec in Canada. They can discuss the fact that the name "Québec" comes from the Algonquin word "Kébec" which means "narrow river." These exercises honor the work of Tuck and Yang whereby we continuously acknowledge the removal of Native inhabitants from their land, as well as our complicity in that historical wrong.

Proficiency Check: Novice learners can write a sentence about where they are from and whose land they occupy. In Spanish, this would be a good use of ser (where you are from) and *estar* (on whose land you sit).

Ask Yourself!

◆ Who were the original inhabitants of the land now owned or occupied by your institution?

◆ Is there ethical engagement with Native students on campus and Native communities today?

◆ What are the legacies of land disenfranchisement of Native communities or other communities in your area, and how have you and/or your institution benefited, e.g., gentrification?

◆ What repair or solidarity-building work has been done with Native communities?

◆ Who leads when you engage with Native communities?

◆ Do you incorporate course content on Indigenous communities, or are they omitted from your curriculum?

◆ Is course content related to Indigenous people authored by Indigenous people?

◆ Do you teach on Indigenous people as historical figures, or modern-day inhabitants who continue to live, thrive, struggle and resist?

Amanda Morris wrote:

> Today, **settler-colonialism** plays out in the erasure of Indigenous presence. American schools do not teach about Native Americans, past or present; when they do, information is often wrong or incomplete. Students are rarely taught about contemporary Native peoples who have survived the settler-colonial process and continue to thrive, create, practice their traditions and live modern lives.
>
> (2019, para 10.)

Including Native content should not oversimplify colonization or take the place of troubling stolen, seized or occupied land; moreover, this content should open the door to conversation, introspection and acknowledgement of the complicated histories and enduring legacies of settler colonialism. Kubota cautions against only referencing settler colonialism in the content of White supremacy. She stated:

> [T]he relationship between non-White settlers and Aboriginal people have been complex largely due to economic struggles for power. Furthermore all settlers of Canada, European or non-European, have sought economic opportunities at the expense of Aboriginal people's lives, land, culture and rights through exploitation, marginalisation and infringement. But not all settlers have been equal; their relations of power have been in flux depending on the local and global political and economic circumstances in history.
>
> (Kubota, 2015, p. 7)

On the Web

- ◆ In the following article, Native parents and educators share how schools still get it wrong. www.learningforjustice.org/magazine/summer-2017/with-and-about-inviting-contemporary-american-indian-peoples-into-the
- ◆ You can access the following website to gain understanding on how to acknowledge Indigenous land ethically and respectfully. https://nativegov.org/a-guide-to-indigenous-land-acknowledgment/
- ◆ This website can be used to locate the original Indigenous inhabitants of your current geographical location. https://native-land.ca/

Geographical Naming: Acknowledgement of Original Inhabitants

> **Proficiency Check:** At novice levels, educators can discuss geography and the original Indigenous names of occupied lands. Educators can scaffold this introduction to reveal celebrations of Native heritage, rituals and practices that have survived over time. Educators might also include a more complex analysis of stolen lands, battles, resistance and genocides. The following example shows that the Native inhabitants of Puerto Rico, los Borinqueños or Taínos, named their island Boriken. Similarly, the Taínos and other Indigenous groups of Haiti first called their island Quisqueya.

In addition to the original names, other ways that students can make the connection to colonialism and settler colonialism is through maps. They can map out the different continents based on colonization. Using words, symbols, colors or flags, students can indicate who colonized the land, and as a result, what languages are now represented. What is/are the official language(s) today? Has/have the official language/s shifted over time? If so, in what context and why?

Many of the countries or regions that speak the languages that we teach are steeped in colonization (based on imperialism). For instance, in a Chinese language classroom it is important to name the fact that China colonized Korea and Taiwan; likewise, in a Portuguese classroom instructors should introduce students to cultures of African countries such as Mozambique and Guinea-Bissau so students can understand the impact of Portuguese colonization in African countries. When discussing occupation, educators should consider external occupations, such as those committed by Europeans on the global south, as well as internal occupations committed by neighboring groups. One example is the history of Haiti and the Dominican Republic.

Educators can present a Venn Diagram so that students can see the history of occupation and its legacies.

Complicated Web of Colonization

Haiti

- Colonized by French
- Language: French, Kreyòl
- National Sport:
- Soccer
- National Religion: Vodou, Catholicism & Protestantism
- One hour behind

- Colonization/ Independence (Haiti from French Imperialists (1804), D.R. from Spain (1821)
- Haitian occupation of D.R. (1822-1844)
- United States occupied Haiti in 1915; Dominican Republic in 1916.
- 1937, Massacre River, Parsley Massacre (Perejil) (Trujillo)

Dominican Republic

- Colonized by Spanish
- Language: Spanish
- National Sport: Baseball
- National Religion: Catholicism
- One hour ahead

Celebrate Survival and Resistance

Another way to honor original inhabitants and minoritized individuals is to celebrate how their cultures have survived and thrived in spite of colonization, imperialism and genocide. Educators must celebrate communities that continue to "create art for resistance, art for (re)membering, art for joy, art for love, art for healing, and art for humanity" (Love, 2019, p. 99). This quote affirms the need to include lessons that serve multiple purposes and that speak to diverse experiences.

Celebratory lessons should not be arbitrary. Educators should incorporate the actual ways in which marginalized communities celebrate their own heritage and legacies of endurance. BIPOC communities and other marginalized groups should serve as a lighthouse for what is deemed celebratory. Not engaging with the communities can result in tokenizing treatment. Many festivals and gatherings of today are rooted in deep cultural connections, resistance and survival. For example, today the Black Garífuna of Central America celebrate the dance ritual called Wanaragua. The dance commemorates a victory over Spanish conquistadors who tried to sexually assault Garífuna women, only to find Garífuna men disguised as women with knives under their dresses. Today, the dance ritual entails Garífuna men dressed as women wearing masks and performing the sacred dances that have survived over the centuries. Other examples follow. Oluo (2019) wrote:

> Race is more than just pain and oppression, it's also culture and history. Personally, my blackness is a history of strength, beauty, and creativity that draws on every day; it is more than the history of the horrors that racism has wrought. My blackness has its own language, its own jokes, its own fashion. My blackness is a community and a family and I'm very grateful for it. Humans are resilient and creative beings, and out of a social construct created to brutalize and oppress, we've managed to create a lot of beauty. We can fight racial oppression while still acknowledging and appreciating that.
>
> (p. 21)

Let's Celebrate!

Indigenous and Tribal People's Convention of 1989 leading to the Declaration of the Rights of Indigenous People	Osun Itaguaí festival celebrating Yoruba heritage and culture in Rio de Janeiro, Brazil	Juneteenth festivals in various parts of USA celebrating enslaved African people's emancipation, liberation and independence
Global pride celebration bringing together pride volunteers from every region of the world		Matwaala South Asian Diaspora Poets Collective to combat South Asian invisibility
Martinique's Carnival celebrating Martinique's history, culture and traditions		Casa Coyolillo festival celebrating Afro-Mexican traditions of Veracruz

Ask Yourself!

◆ What other celebrations of cultural heritage might you include?

◆ How do marginalized people continue to thrive?

On the Web

◆ **Indigenous Convention:** www.ilo.org/global/topics/indigenous-tribal/lang--en/index.htm

◆ **Osun Festival:** https://youtu.be/uWq56gPn-M8

◆ **Juneteenth:** www.tsl.texas.gov/ref/abouttx/juneteenth.html

◆ **Global Pride:** www.globalpride2020.org/

◆ **Matwaala:** www.matwaala.com/about.html

◆ **Martinique's Carnival:** https://us.martinique.org/discover/martiniques-carnival

◆ **Casa Coyolillo Afro-Mestizo:** www.facebook.com/kasa.koyolillo/?fref=ts

---

Activity

Krishauna's students created posters that were called My ____ is dope. *Dope* means awesome, cool or great. In the blank, students inserted my *family* is dope, my *life* is dope, my *partner* is dope, my *sports team* is dope, *blackness* is dope, my *culture* is dope, etc. Students used art supplies, magazine cut outs and other items to illustrate their love of who they are. They then presented these to the class.

Proficiency Check: Novice learners could incorporate a similar sentence using the target language. Since the posters are visuals, students of all proficiencies can engage. Novice learners can use process writing to write the script for what they will present to the class about their posters.

Language and Accent Bias: An Enduring Legacy of Colonization

Chicana, lesbian, feminist, Gloria Anzaldúa popularized the term **linguistic terrorism**. Anzaldúa explained:

> Chicanas who grew up speaking Chicano Spanish have internalized the belief that we speak poor Spanish. It is illegitimate, a bastard language. And because we internalized how our language has been used against us by the dominant culture, we use our language differences against each other.
>
> (1987, p. 38)

In the world language classroom, it is important that instructors acknowledge and respect the various forms of target language expression throughout the target community. This applies to the many variations of words and expressions.

Activity

Normalize variety. Have a bulletin board or slide that has many different expressions about variety such as "variety is the spice of life." Have one word or sentence and have cut outs of all the different ways of saying that word or expression. Be sure to include different regions and communities who speak the target language. See the following English example.

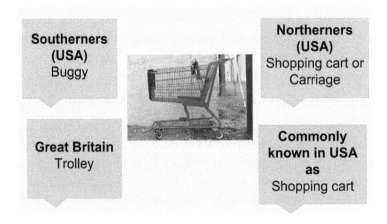

Southerners (USA)
Buggy

Northerners (USA)
Shopping cart or Carriage

Great Britain
Trolley

Commonly known in USA as
Shopping cart

Ask Yourself!

◆ What similar expressions exist in the target language related to variety and difference as a positive attribute?

◆ What are some varieties that you can highlight in your class to demonstrate what Spanish teacher Susan Keener states, "Difference is not bad, different is just different"?

◆ How can you decenter language hierarchies in your classroom?

There should be no hierarchy. A particular word can be used more in a specific region, but that does not make it inferior or superior. The instructor should be cognizant of these nuances, and create an environment where all varieties and accents are valued. Instructors should also affirm the diversities of linguistic expression found in target communities such as African American Vernacular English, Chicanx Spanish, Haitian Kreyòl, Jamaican Patois, etc. Anzaldúa (1987) powerfully expressed:

> So, if you want to really hurt me, talk badly about my language. Ethnic identity is twin skin to linguistic identity – I am my language. Until I can take pride in my language, I cannot take pride in myself. Until I can accept as legitimate Chicano Texas Spanish, Tex-Mex, and all the other languages I speak, I cannot accept the legitimacy of myself. Until I am free to write bilingually and to switch codes without having always to translate, while I still have to speak English or Spanish when I would rather speak Spanglish, and as long as I have to accommodate the English speakers rather than having them accommodate me, my tongue will be illegitimate.
>
> (Anzaldúa, 1987, pp. 39–40)

Accents also produce a form of linguistic diversity. Nigerian-born queer writer Kimberly Joe defines **accent bias** as "the unjustifiable discrimination of individuals who speak a language with an accent" (Joe, 2020, para. 1). Rather, consciously or unconsciously, we often make judgments about accents. Some accents are considered romantic or sexy, while others are considered erudite or cultured. To the contrary, some are considered brute, low class or uneducated. Bias towards different accents is often rooted in microaggressions, stereotypes and implicit bias.

Politics of Accents and Language: For Educators

Is there a variety of accents represented in auditory activities?

Do the accents represent different countries and different ethnic groups? Which accents are included most often?

If teaching Mandarin, are most of the examples from China, or do they also include Hong Kong, Singapore or Taiwan?

If teaching French, in addition to France, are there speakers from Québec, Haiti, Senegal, Mali and Guadeloupe?

Are there magazines, films, etc. from different countries where there are different regionalisms?

Are different accents presented in the classroom in an affirming manner, or as substandard?

Politics of Accents and Language: For Students

What languages did you grow up hearing?

How would you describe your own accent or speech pattern or that of family members?

What stereotypes are associated with those accents or speech patterns?

What experiences have you faced based on your accent or speech pattern?

How do you negotiate, alter, or honor your accent, speech pattern or language?

How likely are you to hear a different language throughout your day?

Microaggressions

Individuals who speak with what is considered a *foreign* accent or vernacular may face **microaggressions**. The term microaggressions was originally coined by African American psychologist Chester M. Pierce, and later expanded upon by Chinese psychologist Derald Wing Sue. Microaggressions are commonplace, daily exchanges that send put-downs or rude messages to members of minority groups. Anyone can commit microaggressions (Sue, 2017). An example of a microaggression is to assume that minoritized individuals were not born in the United States. Microaggressions often result from preconceived notions or stereotypes.

Activity

◆ Ask students to list microaggressions that they have faced. Have students translate them into the target language.

◆ Place signs with microaggressions throughout the classroom.

◆ Some microaggressions may not translate well, and those can be written in English.

◆ After you have displayed the microaggressions throughout the room, give each student about 10 stickers.

◆ Have students place a sticker on all microaggressions that they have heard someone else say, or have said themselves.

◆ Next, ask students to stand under the microaggression that most resonates with them, and have them explain why.

Proficiency Check: Novice speakers can share an emotion in the target language of how the microaggression made them feel, whereas intermediate and advanced speakers can explain in the target language their sentiments more fully.

Stereotypes

The word stereotype is derived from the French adjective *stéréotype*. The etymology of *stéréotype* is from the Greek word "stereos" meaning solid or firm and "typos" meaning impression. Thus, the word refers to a firm impression of an idea or theory. A **stereotype** is an over-generalized belief about a particular group of people. In the practice of stereotyping, there is an assumption that someone/something has certain characteristics or abilities that all members of the group have. An example of a stereotype would be that Asians are good at math and science, or that Latinx individuals are good dancers. Other stereotypes could be that Black men are violent or aggressive. Antiracist world language educators must strive to dismantle stereotypes. One source of microaggressions and stereotypes is implicit bias.

Activity

First, remind students of the classroom guidelines that you have developed in Chapter 1 for healthy discussions. Place an identity on a sheet of paper, board or screen so that all students can see it. Ask students to share some common stereotypes associated with that identity. They can walk around the room and write their responses on the paper. *Be sure to acknowledge that what they write may not be their personal feelings, but we are seeking commonly held beliefs in society.* Then build on that word by adding another descriptor to the word, and continue with the same question. For example, you might start with common stereotypes of *students*, and then move to *male students*, and then move to *female students*, and then move to *Asian students* and then *student athletes*. With each word that you add, a different perspective will surface regarding stereotypes associated with different groups. After the lists are generated, ask discussion questions to unpack the stereotypes further.

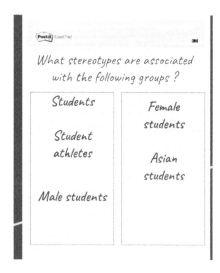

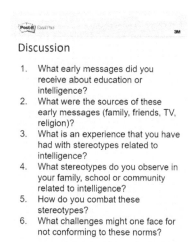

Implicit and Explicit Bias

Also known as **implicit** social cognition or unconscious bias, **implicit bias** refers to the attitudes or stereotypes that affect our understanding, actions and decisions in an unconscious manner. **Explicit bias** is somewhat distinct in that it is a bias that you hold, and you are aware of it. For example, you may be fully aware that you have a bias against a certain political party. An example of implicit bias may manifest in instructors' views on which form of the target language is most pure, valid or respectable.

Since implicit biases are unconscious, they can be particularly damaging when left unchecked. Research shows that, albeit unconscious, our actions (such as microaggressions) and beliefs (such as stereotypes) still follow implicit biases.

Strategies to become aware of and to combat bias are known as **debiasing techniques**. One debiasing technique is to "enlarge your table" by attending events related to difference. In addition to cultural celebrations such as festivals, you should also attend events with panels and guest lecturers who are speaking about their communities from their lived experiences and critical analyses. Establish genuine relationships with people across differences. The more you engage with different social groups, the more awareness you will have about those groups. You should also take advantage of training on bias. Psychologist Carey Morewedge of Boston University found: "...even a single training intervention... can have significant debiasing effects that persist across a variety of contexts affected by the same bias" (Morewedge et al., 2015, p. 137). Additional debiasing techniques follow:

Debiasing Technique	Debiasing Description	Debiasing the World Language Classroom
Know details and not big categories.	The more you get to know people on an individual basis, you will find meaningful connections, which in turn reduce bias.	Have consistent community-building activities for students to get to know each other.
Incorporate counter-stereotypical images.	These are images that go against negative portrayals and negative stereotypes of certain groups. These images present a more positive, diverse or complex view of the social group.	Find images that counter commonly held stereotypes. Have posters/images that show people of color in the fullness and complexities of their lives.

Debiasing Technique	Debiasing Description	Debiasing the World Language Classroom
Stress less.	When stressed, hungry, or sleep deprived people tend to be less sensitive about how they engage with others. Less stress + slow down = less biased.	Teach healthy practices such as social-emotional intelligence, breathing exercises, supply healthy snacks and encourage self-care.
Beware of confirmation bias.	Confirmation bias is when you seek to confirm your biased assumptions. For example, if you feel that heavy people are lazy, when you see a heavy person seated and inactive, you will feel justified in that belief.	Take note of when you feel or display affirmation of your bias. Use statistics, data, evidence, relationships and some of the techniques above to show that the bias is not true, exaggerated, or over-generalized.
Know facts.	Bias can be combated with facts. Learn facts that will dispel myths and media representations of certain groups.	Fill bulletin boards with important facts and diverse portrayals of target cultures and communities, especially underrepresented groups.

On the Web

◆ Educators and their students can join over 5 million people globally who have taken Harvard University's Implicit Associations Test to assess their biases against certain groups. https://implicit.harvard.edu/implicit/

◆ View TedTalk of Verna Myers, Vice-President for Inclusive Strategy at Netflix, titled, How to overcome our biases, walk boldly toward them. www.youtube.com/watch?v=uYyvbgINZkQ

Activity

Consider the following well-known actors. They all have distinct accents. These accents are either their native tongues, or a film portrayal of a certain regionalized manner of speaking.

| Forrest Gump, Alabama | Sofía Vergara, Colombia | Tabitha Brown, North Carolina |

Discussion Questions

1. Discuss the different accents that are associated with each actor.
2. What microaggressions might these actors face based on their accents?
3. What stereotypes are associated with these accents?
4. What biases may individuals hold against people who speak with these accents?
5. What debiasing techniques can be utilized to combat language and accent bias?

Translanguaging and Code Switching

There are several ways that individuals may respond to language and accent bias. One technique is **code-switching**. Courtney L. McCluney, Kathrina Robotham, Serenity Lee, Richard Smith and Myles Durkee wrote in the *Harvard Business Review*: "Broadly, code-switching involves adjusting one's style of speech, appearance, behavior, and expression in ways that will optimize the comfort of others in exchange for fair treatment, quality service, and employment opportunities" (McCluney et al., 2019, para. 3). For example, African

Americans may deviate from African American Vernacular English (AAVE) and speak the language of the academy, also termed standard English. This negotiation may allow them to be received as more professional, educated and possessing more leadership skills. A downside is that code-switching may separate them from their home communities and cause them to be seen as inauthentic or putting on airs.

A second technique is **translanguaging**. Ofelia García (2009), professor of urban, bilingual and Latin American education from the City University of New York, explained: "Translanguaging is the act performed by bilinguals of accessing different linguistic features or various modes of what are described as autonomous languages, in order to maximize communicative potential" (p. 140). The goal of translanguaging is communication, not language itself. Therefore, being able to express oneself while accessing their available linguistic resources may supersede adherence to rigid grammar rules and linguistic codes. One example of translanguaging is Spanglish, a blending of Spanish and English. Language educators may have concerns that translanguaging will interfere with the language goals of the course. Given that the home-school-community triad is a foundational tenet of a culturally responsive language classroom, we invite educators to affirm the language of their students' communities.

Educators should present home languages and vernaculars as valuable linguistic tools and resources. International Baccalaureate Spanish teacher of the Semiahmoo Secondary School, Adriana Ramírez shared:

> The approach most institutions use to teaching languages is also an imposition of White supremacy. The grammar approach is not an equitable way of teaching languages. It is geared to a small percentage of the population. The way we are told/taught we are supposed to teach languages and grade/assess our students is also racist.
>
> (personal communication, July 5, 2021)

Language educators can combat deficit-based approaches by expressing and modeling how rich it is to be able to use language in such creative ways to enhance communication. In so doing, this approach will not devalue the home language. Also, present code-switching and translanguaging as complex linguistic systems just as you would the target language. As educators, "[y]ou can then make a distinction between your classroom approach to languages and the language resources the students will need to use in exams" (What is Translanguaging? 2016, para. 12). Translanguaging and code-switching allow for greater flexibility for students to access classroom content while also honoring the language of the home.

Activity

Give a list of common idiomatic expressions in the target language and invite students to share a comparable expression in their home language. Also, point out the structure (linguistic, historical or cultural elements) of the expressions so that the analysis is complex and not flat and one-dimensional.

	Spanish Idiom	AAVE Idiom
Idiom: With friends like that, who needs enemies	*Más vale solo que mal acompañado.*	I can do bad all by myself.
Structure	Sentence structure incorporates comparison (*más/que* construction).	Sentence structure incorporates the affirmative voice (can-do statement).

Offer students the opportunity to create poetry or prose using both their home language and the target language. For example, in her poem *Speak White*, French Canadian poet Michèle Lalonde (1968) combined English and French to emphasize how language is racialized. In his poem, *Mi Chiquita*, Afro-Cuban poet Nicolás Guillén (1930) incorporated phonetic spellings to demonstrate diverse pronunciations. *Mi Chiquita* should also be examined for gender norms.

Nicolás Guillén, Mi Chiquita (1930)
Afro-Cuban Poet

Mi chiquita
La chiquita que yo tengo
tan negra como e͟,
no la cambio po ninguna,
po ninguna otra mujé͟.

Ella la͟ba, plancha, cose,
y sobre to, caballero,
¡como co͟sina!

Si la bienen a bucá͟
pa͟ bailá͟,
pa͟ comé,
ella me tiene que llebá͟,
o traé͟.

Ella me di͟se: mi santo,
tú no me puede dejá;
buca͟mé,
buca͟mé,
buca͟mé,
pa͟ go͟sá͟.

The little gal that I have
As Black as she is
I would not change her
Not for any other gal

She washes, irons, sews, and
More than anything, man can she cook.

If you come to look for her
To dance or
To eat
She has to take me
or bring me
She says to me, my saint,
You can't leave me
Look for me
Look for me
To have a little fun

On the Web

◆ See Black Entertainment Television documentary titled 'Black English': How AAVE developed from slave resistance and African dialects in *The Breakdown*. www.youtube.com/watch?v=K7FIky7wplI

◆ See The costs of code-switching in *Harvard Business Review*. https://hbr.org/2019/11/the-costs-of-codeswitching

Ask Yourself!

◆ What messages have you received (conscious or unconscious) regarding home languages?

◆ What have you been socialized to believe is the value added and/or value lost with regard to home languages?

◆ How might you affirm home languages in the antiracist world language classroom?

◆ How might you incorporate home languages into the language classroom?

◆ For the language that you teach, do you incorporate the diverse varieties of that language (for example, English as well as AAVE and Patois)?

◆ Do you educate your students on additional languages that are spoken by target communities? For example, speakers of French may also speak Haitian Kreyòl or Wolof. Speakers of Portuguese may also speak Makhuwa. Speakers of Spanish may also speak Garífuna.

Anti-Blackness and Anti-Darkness

Along with valuing the language of the home, educators must also value the diverse races and ethnicities that make up the mosaic of our classrooms. Shifting from teachers to students, Bettina Love offers the following analysis regarding anti-blackness. **Anti-blackness** is the unfair, inequitable, discriminatory, racist, disenfranchised treatment and policies that further exacerbate the oppression of Black students. Bettina Love (2019) characterizes **anti-darkness** as bias against Black and Brown children. She also notes that anti-darkness and anti-blackness can occur whether dark children are in the room or not. These racist ideals harm all children, regardless of race.

Bettina Love (2019, p.22) wrote:

> The conditions that preserve dark suffering are the result of hundreds of years and multiple continents' commitment to creating and maintaining destructive, insidious, racist ideals that uphold White supremacy and anti-Blackness. We like to think that education is untouched by White supremacy, White rage, and anti-Blackness, that educators are somehow immune to perpetuating dark suffering. But education from the outset was built on White supremacy, anti-Blackness, and sexism.

Educators must not present target cultures as monoliths. It is important that students understand not only the diversity of target communities, but also how they treat and portray marginalized members of their communities.

Manifestations of Anti-BIPOC in Target Cultures

Oftentimes the way that certain bodies are perceived in target cultures can present a negative portrayal of those groups. Ibram X. Kendi explained that **bodily racism** is perceiving certain racialized bodies as more animal-like and violent than others. Some examples of anti-BIPOC regarding bodily racism follow. How do these images demonstrate or respond to anti-blackness or Anti-BIPOC?

Donald Trump's comments during the 2016 Presidential Campaign: "When Mexico sends its people, they're not sending their best … They're sending people that have lots of problems, and they're bringing those problems with us. They're bringing drugs. They're bringing crime. They're rapists. And some, I assume, are good people" (Phillips, 2017).

Sandy's Import candy depicts Black people as primitive.

Ask Yourself!

Review the images that relate to various target cultures. Respond to the following discussion questions.

◆ What messages do you receive from these images?
◆ What do you surmise is the thought or intention behind the images?
◆ Where do you think these messages originated?
◆ What is the impact of portraying certain groups in this manner?
◆ What other examples of bodily racism have you observed in society, television, media, social media, gifs, memes, etc.?
◆ How might we combat these depictions?

Below is a list of practices that promote racist policies and behaviors as well as antiracist practices that combat racism. Reflect on which aspects of the chart speak to your experiences. Also, reflect on how you might raise your consciousness, acquire skills and access resources to move your language classroom from racist practices to antiracist practices. The following chart is meant to be a reflective rather than an exhaustive list.

Manifestations of Anti-blackness and Anti-darkness		
Category	*Racist Practices Include...*	*Antiracist Practices Include...*
One and Done	◆ One and done approach such as one lesson on antiracism, or one diversity training.	◆ Antiracist lessons that are evenly embedded into and distributed throughout the curriculum.
Omission	◆ No discussion of race, ethnicity, racism, colorism, antiracism or the experiences of racialized people.	◆ An enthusiastic, structured and well-planned incorporation and assessment of race, ethnicity, racism, colorism, antiracism and the experiences of racialized people.

Manifestations of Anti-blackness and Anti-darkness		
Category	*Racist Practices Include…*	*Antiracist Practices Include…*
Tragedy	◆ Presenting a group of individuals only in terms of their oppression.	◆ Acknowledging that all people lead complicated and complex lives, and are more than a single story.
Acquiescence	◆ No presentation of resistance in the face of oppression.	◆ An acknowledgement that it is unethical to present a history of oppression without also presenting how oppressed people have resisted throughout history and today.
Representation	◆ Very few or no representations of course content that visibly shows people of color. ◆ Few to no faculty and staff of color represented in the language classroom.	◆ Incorporating content that is highly representative of diverse racial communities and experiences. ◆ Hiring BIPOC as language faculty and staff members and/or guest lecturers. *Note:* To include BIPOC content while excluding BIPOC is an illusion of inclusion.
Credit Hoarding	◆ Omitting content written by BIPOC. ◆ Denying and omitting BIPOC contributions to the world language discipline. ◆ Taking credit for BIPOC thought, ideas and contributions.	◆ Incorporating the writings, films, art, essays, books, presentations, etc. of BIPOC. ◆ Actively demonstrating how BIPOC have enhanced and shifted the discipline of world languages and contributed to literature, science, history, national narratives, social change and more.

Manifestations of Anti-blackness and Anti-darkness		
Category	*Racist Practices Include…*	*Antiracist Practices Include…*
Credit Hoarding (continued)		◆ Inviting BIPOC to give presentations and guest lectures. ◆ Inviting BIPOC to publish and contribute to research projects and publishable works.
Social Justice God	◆ Incorporating social justice to the exclusion of antiracism.	◆ Acknowledging that social justice is akin to antiracism, but it is not its equivalent. ◆ Showing how social justice and antiracism intersect and how they are distinct. *Note:* The absence of this distinction can give social justice educators and leaders a pass to not address race in world languages.

Ask Yourself!

◆ What other categories and practices might you add to this list?

References

Anzaldúa, G. (1987). *Borderlands la frontera: The new mestiza*. Aunt Lute Books.

García, O. (2009). Education, multilingualism and translanguaging in the 21st century. In A. Mohanty, M. Panda, R. Phillipson & T. Skutnabb-Kangas (Eds.), *Social Justice through Multilingual Education* (pp. 128–145). Multilingual Matters. https://doi.org/10.21832/9781847691910-011

Guillén, N. (1930). *Mi chiquita*. In Poeticous. www.poeticous. com/guillen/mi-chiquita?locale=es

Guillén, N. (1931). *Caña*. In Poemas del alma. www.poemas-del-alma.com/nicolas-guillen-cana.htm

Joe, K. (Executive Producer). (2020, January 17). *Accent bias (No. 9)*. Audio podcast episode. In *Medium*. https://kimberlyjoe. medium.com/accent-bias-75b566ab5da4

Kendi, I.X. (2019). *How to be an antiracist*. Random House.

Lalonde, M. (1968). *Speak white*. In Dormira jamais. http:// dormirajamais.org/speak-white/

Longley, R. (2021, February 16). *What is Colonialism? Definition and Examples*. ThoughtCo. www.thoughtco.com/colonialism-definition-and-examples-5112779

Love, B.L. (2019). *We want to do more than survive: Abolitionist teaching and the pursuit of educational freedom*. Beacon Press.

McCluney, C.L., Robotham, K., Lee, S., Smith, R., & Durkee, M. (2019, November 15). *The costs of code-switching. Harvard Business Review*. https://hbr.org/2019/11/the-costs-of-codeswitching

Morewedge, C.K., Yoon, H., Scopelliti, I, Symborski, C.W. , Korris, J.H., & Kassam, K.S. (2015). Debiasing decisions: Improved decision making with a single training intervention. *Policy Insights from the Behavioral and Brain Sciences* (2)1, 129–140.

Morris, A. (2019, January 22). *What is Settler-Colonialism?* Learning for Justice. www.learningforjustice.org/magazine/ what-is-settlercolonialism

National Center for Education Statistics. (2018). Bachelor's degrees conferred by postsecondary institutions, by race/ ethnicity and field of study: 2017–18. https://nces.ed.gov/ programs/digest/d18/tables/dt18_322.30.asp

Oluo, I. (2019). *So you want to talk about race*. Seal Press.

Phillips, A. (2017, June 16). 'They're rapists.' President Trump's campaign launch speech two years later, annotated. *Washington Post*. www.washingtonpost.com/news/the-fix/wp/ 2017/06/16/theyre-rapists-presidents-trump-campaign-launch-speech-two-years-later-annotated/

Racial Equity Tools. (n.d.). System of White Supremacy and White Privilege. www.racialequitytools.org/resources/Fundamentals/Core-Concepts/System-of-White-Supremacy-and-White-Privilege

Sandronsky, S. (2005, November 23). *An Interview with David Roediger*. MROnline. https://mronline.org/2005/11/23/an-interview-with-david-roediger/

Sue, D.W. (2017). Microaggressions and "Evidence": Empirical or Experiential Reality? *Perspectives on Psychological Science*, 12(1), 170–172.

Tuck, E. & Yang, K.W. (2012). Decolonization is not a Metaphor. *Decolonization: Indigeneity, Education & Society*, 1(1), 1–40.

Watzke, J. (2003). *Lasting change in foreign language education: A historical case for change in national policy*. Praeger Publishing.

What is translanguaging? (2016, July 26). *EAL Journal*. https://ealjournal.org/2016/07/26/what-is-translanguaging/

3

Setting the Stage for the Antiracist Classroom

We must first educate ourselves, we must learn, unlearn, read and study. We must see first, in order to teach our students to open their eyes and see. We must disrupt the status quo with the materials we use and what we choose to center in our classes. We must have difficult conversations with our students. We must give them tools to see, analyze and change the world. I love a word that I learned from Paulo Freire's Pedagogy of the Oppressed: PRAXIS = Reflection + Action.

(Adriana Ramírez, Spanish, Semiahmoo
Secondary School)

This chapter focuses on the antiracist world language classroom, educator and student. The first stage of antiracism begins with self. For this reason, we will call upon educators and students to examine their dispositions and proclivities as they relate to race, racism and antiracism. We will present identity-based activities that focus on intersecting identities of race, class, gender, sexuality, national origin, religion and more. Then we will present community-building activities that enable students to build relationships with their peers, and openly discuss differences and

DOI: 10.4324/9781003218265-4

similarities. Furthermore, we will present strategies for reframing existing curricula with an antiracist approach. These approaches will set the stage to incorporate the topic of antiracism across languages, levels and proficiencies.

Action Steps for the Antiracist Educator

> ### *On the Web*
>
> ◆ How to be an antiracist educator by Dena Simmons. www.ascd.org/el/articles/how-to-be-an-antiracist-educator

Be an Antiracist Educator By Dena Simmons	
1: Engage in vigilant self-awareness	**2**: Acknowledge racism and white supremacy
3: Teach representative history	**4**: Talk about race with students
5: When you see racism, do something	

Educator & diversity scholar Dena Simmons, formerly of the Yale University Center for Emotional Intelligence, designed concrete and tangible action steps for how to be an antiracist educator. The first action is to engage in **vigilant self-awareness**. Engaging in vigilant self-awareness will allow educators to check their implicit biases. Simmons (2019) wrote, "Engage in vigilant awareness of your implicit bias to ensure that you are not part of the problem, too" (para. 9). Since some biases are unconscious and may contradict one's espoused beliefs, reflective exercises can help educators to assess their attitudes toward certain individuals or groups. Bias is often exacerbated by privileged identities.

Critical race scholars Richard Delgado and Jean Stefancic (2017) defined **privilege** as a "right or advantage, often unwritten, conferred on some people but not others" (p. 182). Given our multiple identities, who we are also impacts how we teach and how we view and engage our students. Simmons (2019) concluded, "If we do not know our power, we can abuse it unintentionally or fail to leverage it toward antiracism" (para. 3).

Simmons' second action step for the antiracist educator is to **acknowledge racism and White supremacy**. Many language educators omit the topic of race altogether. Some are open to discussing race, but not racism. Others are open to discussing racism, but not White supremacy. Educators must combat **color-blind racism** or color evasiveness where they disregard, downplay or omit the impact of race and ethnicity in society. The third action step is to teach **representative history**. Representative history seeks to include omitted voices and to unearth suppressed histories and stories. This reimagined history centers the fuller narrative of racialized experiences and trauma, but also includes how people of color have resisted and triumphed in the face of racism. Action four is to **talk about race** with your students. Chinese history professor at Guilford College, Zhihong Chen, actively engages her students in discussions of race. For example, she compares the Chinese Exclusion Act of 1882 to the exclusion felt by many Black and Brown individuals in the United States.

Not addressing race sends a message of silence and apathy. French teacher, Christen Campbell remarked:

> The biggest attribute an antiracist teacher can offer is to talk about race. Admit to not being perfect, not knowing everything, but if you ignore the things that happen on a day-to-day basis, we then are complicit in the racist actions of others.
> (personal communication, June 30, 2021)

Action five is **when you see racism, do something**. Simmons (2019) wrote, "To combat racism, consider how the academic resources, policies, admissions, hiring, grading, and behavior management practices at your school might be racist" (para. 9).

Educators will need to interrogate their practices and school policies, and ask critical questions. Our students' success is dependent upon our introspection and action. Use the following two
charts to self-assess your antiracist practices, sentiments and
attitudes.

Self-Assessment of an Antiracist Educator				
Use the chart below to assess to what extent you have engaged in antiracist actions.				
Actions of an antiracist educator	If you answered no, explain why you have not engaged in these actions.	If you answered yes, explain how you have engaged in these actions.	List the resources or support that you incorporate into your antiracism journey.	List the resources that you lack or need to support your antiracism journey.
1. I engage in vigilant self-awareness.	No (Why not?)	Yes (How?)	I incorporate…	I lack/need…
2. I acknowledge racism and White supremacy.	No (Why not?)	Yes (How?)		
3. I teach representative history.	No (Why not?)	Yes (How?)		
4. I talk about race with students.	No (Why not?)	Yes (How?)		
5. When I see racism occurring, I do something.	No (Why not?)	Yes (How?)		
6. Would you consider yourself an antiracist educator?	No (Why not?)	Yes (How?)		

Adapted from Dena Simmons' framework for *How to be an Antiracist Educator* (2019).

Racial Attitudes Assessment		
The following are quotes from three racial justice scholars and educators. Read their quotes, and consider the reflective questions that follow.		
Assess your racial attitude toward others	**Assess your allyship**	**Assess how you view members of your own group**
"Specifically, educators need to address their own **racial attitudes**, beliefs, and expectations as they relate to their students of color as well as their White students" (Singleton and Linton, 2005, p. 73). **Book: *Courageous conversations about race* (Singleton & Linton, 2005)**	"I believe that **White progressives** cause the most daily damage to people of color" (DiAngelo, 2018, p. 5). **Book: *White fragility* (DiAngelo, 2018)**	"It was important for me to assess the **negative stereotypes** that I had internalized about my own race" (Kemp, 2016, pp. 33–37). **Book: *Say the wrong thing* (Kemp, 2016)**

Racial Attitudes Assessment		
Ask Yourself:	**Ask Yourself:**	**Ask Yourself:**
1. How do I view my White students (consider intersectionality, i.e., class, gender, etc.)?	1. To which communities do I consider myself an ally? Why? How?	1. What early messages did I receive about other racial/ethnic groups?
2. How do I view my students of color (assets/deficits) (break this category up by race, i.e., Black, Latinx, Asian…)?	2. How would these communities know that I am in fact an ally?	2. What early messages did I receive about my own racial/ethnic group?
3. How do I define my best students, and what do they look like?	3. What members of that community have affirmed me as their ally, or is the title self-imposed?	3. What derogatory names or stereotypes are associated with members of my race/ethnicity?
4. What factors impact my grading?	4. How am I continuing to learn and grow as an ally?	4. How have those derogatory views impacted me?
5. In my school, who is overrepresented in honors and Advanced Placement programs?	5. How do I accept critique or feedback from the communities that I claim to support?	5. What derogatory names or stereotypes have I used when referencing members of my own race/ethnicity?
6. Who is overrepresented in disciplinary actions?	6. How do I show up for these communities or participate in these communities?	6. How do I see myself as similar to other members of my race/ethnicity?
7. Whose neighborhoods or cultural events do I frequent?	7. How do I allow space to hear from individuals of these communities?	7. How do I see myself as different from members of my race/ethnicity?
8. Which students are associated with good or bad neighborhoods, and how does that impact my perceptions?	8. Do I advocate *for* these communities or *with* these communities?	8. What positive or negative experiences have I had with students/people of color and with White students/people?
9. With whose parents do my paths cross in the community (church, events, sports, etc.)?	9. Is my advocacy private (behind the scenes), public, or both?	

Racial Attitudes Assessment		
10. What can I do to address my own racial attitudes, beliefs and expectations as they relate to students of color and White students?	10. What can I do to become an effective ally?	9. How have these experiences impacted my engagement with members of those communities? 10. What are some concrete actions I can take to erase these internalized negative stereotypes?

Setting up the Antiracist Classroom

Take a moment to look around your classroom. Respond to the following questions.

1. What do you see?
2. Who is represented?
3. Who/What is missing?
4. How is the classroom configured?
5. How would students and visitors know that you are an antiracist educator?
6. What are two things you can do to make sure others know you are an antiracist educator?

Now review your textbook, supplementary resources, online programs, lesson plans, grade book, units of study and assignments. Respond to the same questions as above. See chapters four and five for examples of antiracist daily lessons and units.

Our classrooms tell a story. When students enter our spaces, they must see themselves represented. Be intentional about the visuals that you select for bulletin boards and other classroom displays. Ensure that different races, ethnicities and nationalities, body sizes, genders, people with dis/abilities and other identities are visible. We recommend that language educators see their **classrooms as a canvas**. Which representations are included? Who is controlling the paintbrush?

High school Spanish teacher, Tamara Hughes Akinbo in North Carolina has the outside door of her classroom festively decorated in the colors and emblems of her alma maters. A sign on the door of her classroom reads, "I graduated from Winston-Salem State University with a Bachelor's degree in Spanish, and from Wake Forest University with a Master's degree in Spanish Education. Want to know more? Ask me!" Winston-Salem State University is a historically Black university whereas Wake Forest University is predominantly White. This entrance to her classroom immediately gives her students insights into her language journey, and her diverse academic experiences. Her decorative, yet informative entrance invites students into her space, and opens the door to any questions that they may have about her journey or their futures.

The door is a prelude to the inclusion that flows inside of her classroom. Upon entering Ms. Akinbo's classroom, she has a bulletin board with images of famous Spanish speakers who represent diverse communities in the Spanish-speaking world. Above each image she has a caption in Spanish that reads, "My name is _____. I speak Spanish, and I am from_____." Ms. Akinbo was intentional about including Spanish speakers of different races, ethnicities and nationalities.

We recommend that educators pass the paintbrush to their students. To bring students' voices into the classroom, have a canvas space that is set apart just for them. Teachers can use bulletin boards, white boards, chalk boards or post-its for students to leave messages that represent their identities. Teachers can provide a simple prompt such as, "Who are you?"; "What do you hope to receive from this class?", or "What matters to you?" Teachers can change the sayings every few weeks to make space for others. Examples follow.

Proficiency Check: These sayings can be written in English or the target language.

The Classroom as Canvas

When students enter your classroom, the space matters. Consider when you visit a museum: typically there is something outside that represents the focus of the museum before you ever step inside. Once inside, from the front of the building to the back, you will be inculcated with visuals and text that speak to the larger experience of the content of the museum. Your classroom can also serve as a canvas that engages students, allows them to see themselves reflected and challenges their curiosities. In studio art there is a term called white space.

White space is essentially blank space on a canvas that is underused, not engaged and serves no purpose. In essence, it is wasted space. That being said, be sensitive to diverse cognitive needs of students whereby less may be more. For example, you do not want to overstimulate students with attention deficit and hyperactivity disorder. Consider how to strategically utilize your space. When we honor cultures in our classrooms we also demonstrate our respect for target and home communities. Wolof professor Marie Correa-Fernandes of the University of Kansas stated, "[A]n antiracist world language classroom could mean for instance when teaching culture to not make fun of artifacts or cultural items that represent the culture of the target language" (personal communication, July 8, 2021). Our displaying of cultural items is a great way to model respect to our students.

> ### *Ask Yourself!*
> ◆ What will students see when entering your classroom?
> ◆ Whom do the bulletin boards represent?
> ◆ What images or representations are most prevalent?
> ◆ What images or representations are missing?
> ◆ Which geographical areas are most visible?
> ◆ What is on your door?
> ◆ When seated, entering or exiting, where will the students' attention be most often directed, and what do they see?
> ◆ Where do students see you, the teacher, represented in the classroom?

Virtual Teachers and Floaters

We recognize that for some schools and districts, having your own classroom is a luxury. Here are some tips for those who do not have full ownership or agency over their space.

Tips for Inclusive Representation when Floating or Teaching Online	
Art in print or online	Include as many diverse visuals as possible in your handouts and lessons. South Asian professor Sonalini Sapra from India adds the artwork of marginalized artists to her syllabus as the header. She highlights those who depict social justice or antiracist themes. She strategically uses images as headers either in addition to words or to replace the words. The images then serve as a teaching tool.
Culture Box	If floating, carry a culture box with you to each class that includes significant cultural artifacts (see the Culture Box Examples that follow).

Tips for Inclusive Representation when Floating or Teaching Online	
Students as Cultural Bridges	Ask students to bring cultural artifacts for show and tell. If you cannot bring culture to the students, they can bring it to you.
Culture through Content	Demonstrate your appreciation for culture by incorporating diverse voices and diverse experiences into your instruction. Let your content be a litmus test for inclusion.
The Image Test	Biology professor Rebecca Dunn tests her level of inclusion by adding the portraits of every author that will be included in her course. Not only do the images serve as an accountability check for her, but also as a visual representation of inclusion for her students.
Webpages	Use your webpage to show what you value. Uplift your commitment to all learners. This may be done with links to antiracist supplementary materials such as videos, articles, etc.
Virtual Spaces	Give students an antiracist theme and ask them to come to class with a zoom background that represents that theme.

Gloria Ladson-Billings (1995) defines the term culturally responsive pedagogy as the "dynamic or synergistic relationship between home/community culture and school culture" (p. 467). Fill your classroom spaces with **culturally relevant** objects. These objects should not be random or arbitrary, but should represent the target language or the home-school-community alliance.

Our goal is to bring the people, products and practices indicative of diverse communities into the classroom space. To achieve this goal, we must engage and understand the communities that we teach. Ladson-Billings (1995) wrote, "By observing the students in their home/community environment, teachers were able to include aspects of the students' cultural environment in the organization and instruction of the classroom" (p. 467). The following are examples of possibilities.

Starting a Conversation about Race

The Program on Intergroup Relations at the University of Michigan recommends that educators first engage in *group beginnings* in order to establish and build relationships with students. Group beginnings are activities and dialogues that forge relationships and enable peers to get to know each other better. We have adapted this model to an antiracist framework. Multicultural scholar, Lisa Delpit (2006) wrote, "[I]f we are to be successful at educating diverse children we must take the time to get to know our students" (pgs. 182–183).

Educators should take the first few weeks of class to engage in deliberate community-building activities with their students. These activities will be key to incorporating antiracist lessons later in the term. There are a number of community-building exercises that educators can offer. We presented the framework for engaging in race-based conversations in the Introduction and we will now remind you of those stages and expand upon each one.

Four Stages of Intergroup Dialogue

Stage 1	Group Beginnings: Forming and Building Relationships
Stage 2	Exploring the Nature of Social Identity
Stage 3	Exploring and Discussing Hot Topics
Stage 4	Action Planning and Alliance Building

THE PROGRAM ON INTERGROUP RELATIONS
UNIVERSITY OF MICHIGAN

Stage 1: Build Community

Here is an example of a community building activity.

Coffee Shop Activity

Students can give the presentation below either face to face or they can upload a video, audio, or slideshow if learning virtually. Assign a few classmates to respond to their peers' presentations. Students might ask a question or make a comment regarding what they want to know, or what they learned from the presentations. Instructors should also engage in this activity so that students get a glimpse into their lives as well.

- ◆ State your name. *Me llamo Lourdes.*
- ◆ Include a picture or item that is meaningful to you. *Esta foto es de mi madre.*
- ◆ Where do you feel at home? *Me gusta estar en mi casa en Chicago.*
- ◆ List a few hobbies and interests. *Yo miro las telenovelas.*
- ◆ Tell us something interesting about you. *Yo tengo tres perros.*
- ◆ Include a photo of yourself in your presentation and a map of your hometown. *En esta foto estoy en la playa con mi familia. Este es un mapa de mi ciudad, Chicago.*

Proficiency Check: At novice proficiency levels, students can answer these questions in the target language by using one complete sentence (see previous examples). Their responses might incorporate present tense conjugations, the verbs to be, demonstrative pronouns, specific vocabulary such as family words, etc. Even at novice proficiency levels, students will gain valuable insights into their classmates' lives, backgrounds and experiences. At higher proficiency levels, students can respond to more interrogative words, such as *how* or *why*, to offer further insights and opportunities for greater language production. For example:

◆ State your name *and tell what your name means or the story behind your name.*

◆ Include a picture or item that is meaningful to you, *and explain why.*

◆ Where do you feel at home, *and why?*

◆ List a few hobbies and interests, *and explain why you enjoy them.*

◆ Tell us something interesting about you, *and mention how people typically respond when they learn about this.*

Culture Box Activity

The Culture Box is another activity that can help with community building. Students bring a box to class in which they enclose three items that represent them or that are meaningful to them. Students are also encouraged to decorate the box itself or bring a container that adds meaning to the presentation. Students will work in small groups to share and to discuss their boxes and their contents. Here are some examples of how the students can discuss their culture boxes in the target language at the novice level.

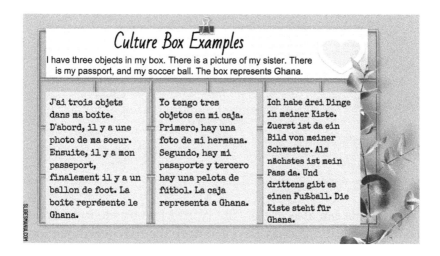

Culture Box Examples

I have three objects in my box. There is a picture of my sister. There is my passport, and my soccer ball. The box represents Ghana.

J'ai trois objets dans ma boîte. D'abord, il y a une photo de ma soeur. Ensuite, il y a mon passeport, finalement il y a un ballon de foot. La boîte représente le Ghana.	Yo tengo tres objetos en mi caja. Primero, hay una foto de mi hermana. Segundo, hay mi pasaporte y tercero hay una pelota de fútbol. La caja representa a Ghana.	Ich habe drei Dinge in meiner Kiste. Zuerst ist da ein Bild von meiner Schwester. Als nächstes ist mein Pass da. Und drittens gibt es einen Fußball. Die Kiste steht für Ghana.

Stage 2: Exploring the Nature of Social Identity

Identity Card Projects

Using the framework of the Race Card Project (see On the Web section that follows), students will use descriptive words to describe their identities. So that students can incorporate identities including race, but not limited to race, we have modified the Race Card Project to incorporate intersectionality. We expanded the title to the Identity Card Project so that students have the opportunity to include multiple identities. Instructions follow. Students will complete the outline in the example below to map out parts of their identities. They should place their name or likeness in the center. Students will write in their race or ethnicity. Students will then select six additional words or phrases that describe various aspects of their identity. These descriptions may relate to other intersecting identities such as class, gender, sexuality, religion, hobbies, etc. Next, students will discuss their descriptions in small groups.

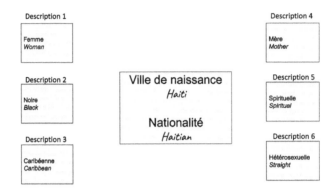

Students can also use the Six Word Memoir site to complete a similar activity. Classes can even have their six-word memoirs published in a book. Like the Race Card Project, the memoirs are accessible for all language levels.

On the Web

◆ View the Race card project on this website: https://theracecardproject.com

◆ View the Six word memoir on this website: www.sixwordmemoirs.com/

Identity Card Discussion Questions

1. Select words or phrases that you are comfortable sharing.
2. Why did you choose those descriptions?
3. What makes you proud of your identity?
4. What are some challenges associated with your identity?
5. What stereotypes are associated with your identity?
6. How do you navigate those perceptions or stereotypes?
7. What do you wish people knew about you or members of your group?
8. What is a question, comment, or assumption that you often encounter?

9. Where did you grow up, and how has your community impacted your identity or experience?

Proficiency Check: The identity card activity is accessible for novice proficiency levels as it only requires six words, and students do not have to form a complete sentence. The discussion of the students' descriptions may occur in the target language, or it may need to occur in English. Teachers can offer process writing for students to formulate discussion points in the target language. Students can use the six descriptions to create sentences, proverbs, sayings, word art and more. Students may simply write out their responses, or they can design their own identity cards using as much creativity as the imagination will allow. Identity cards may mimic identification cards, passports, or art. Examples follow.

GUILFORD
COLLEGE

IDENTITY CARD

Baltimore, MD
Identity: Latino, Male
Student

"Brown and Proud; First generation student."

Exel Valle Estrada
He/him/his

GUILFORD
COLLEGE

IDENTITY CARD

Baltimore, MD
Identity: Woman of Color
Student, BSU President

"Blessed. Resilient. Gorgeous.
Intelligent. Creative.
Sensational."

Celene Warren
She/her/hers

Stage 3: Exploring and Discussing Hot Topics

Hot topics might encompass many areas. One example of a hot topic is the discussion of racism. One form of racism is **invisibility**. Panamanian scholar, Juan Rios Vegas wrote:

> If we review the pages of the textbooks that are used in the institutions of our country [Panamá], we will notice that there are very few images of the Black population. How many writers make the effort to ensure that the ample gamut of races and ethnicities of the country are reflected in their texts?
>
> (in Hines-Gaither, 2015, p. 138)

World language textbooks in the United States also fall into this category. For example, there is a tendency to view French from the perspective of France. In addition to having the traditional representation of French speakers who are from Paris, Lyon, Marseilles or Montréal, instructors should present individuals from Dakar, Lomé, Ouagadougou or Bangui with common names such as Fatou, Amina, Mohammed and Oumar. This inclusion will make students more aware that French speakers are not limited to France. Educators can use an infographic or bulletin board to show the diversity of the francophone world.

Establishing an antiracist classroom will require some heavy lifting in the beginning, but that should not be a deterrent.

Infographic Activity

Students can research the populations, races and ethnicities of the francophone world and represent them through an infographic or a collective bulletin board. Students can work alone or in groups. They might include demographics based on geographical regions, race and ethnicity, history, tourist attractions, foods, cultural products, music, scientists, sports, key figures and more.

> I think what keeps teachers from doing this is that it requires more work. However, once you establish that it is important to incorporate the entire francophone world, students start initiating this work on their own, where they independently chose Congo, Haiti or Morocco. Resources can sometimes be harder to find--but social media has been a huge library for global content.
>
> (Christen Campbell, personal communication, June 30, 2021)

The following example illuminates the need for infographics to supplement our texts. One French textbook lists well-known French personalities ranging from the famous Mona Lisa painting to explorer Jacques Cousteau, French philosopher Voltaire, scientist Marie Curie and French president Charles de Gaulle. All of these prominent figures are French and White.

There is only one Black male that is represented in the entire chapter. He is a well-known soccer player. While the White French figures represent an array of fields and genres, there is a **single story** or a one-dimensional representation of Black people. By having no other representations of Black figures, the textbook is falling into the stereotype of Blacks being famous only because of their athletic abilities. Teachers should incorporate famous people of color from France and other French-speaking countries who represent diverse fields, including but not limited to sports and musicians.

Finally, we call upon educators to create the conditions of learning whereby racialized lessons and discussions are evenly integrated into the language classroom. We encourage instructors to honor celebratory months such as Hispanic/Latinx Heritage Month, Black History Month, Asian Heritage Month, Native American Heritage Month and others. These months most often resulted from the advocacy work of BIPOC and marginalized individuals who resisted the omission of their heritage. While honoring these months, we also call for educators to continue to include antiracist content throughout the school year. This ongoing inclusion can be an important element of an antiracist classroom.

The Danger of a Single-Story Activity

Pre-Viewing Activity: French professor Marie-Angèle Kingué of Bucknell University gives her students a blank map of the African continent and the United States. Students fill their maps with anything that comes to mind that represents the geographical regions. They can write words or draw pictures in the target language or English. Students often write perceptions and conditions of the respective locations, landmarks, famous people, symbols, etc. Kingué does not censure their ideas—she allows them to flow freely, even if some are problematic. She anticipates some imbalanced perspectives. For example, she may clarify that Africa is a continent made up of many countries, and not a single country. She then uses the students' maps to spark conversations about perceptions in small groups or as a class. Kingué may use the students' maps to design follow-up lessons to clarify a misconception, or she may incorporate a film, reading, guest speaker, or provide further resources. Marie Correa-Fernandes, Wolof professor from the University of Kansas, wrote "[e]ducators should strive to be culturally aware towards the target language and the culture of their students to avoid misconceptions, and to help students understand that across the oceans there are great things as well" (personal communication, July 8, 2021).

> ### *On the Web*
> ◆ Show the Ted Talk of Nigerian feminist author, Chimamanda Adichie titled The danger of a single story, which has been watched by over 9 million people. www.youtube.com/watch?v=D9Ihs241zeg

Proficiency Check: This Ted Talk is in English, and therefore not accessible to all languages and proficiency levels. Although the speech is not in the target language, it is far reaching in terms of its global significance. Since the video is in English, we recommend holding the post-viewing discussion in English.

Post-Viewing Activity: Using the questions below, students can discuss the informative points made by Adichie in her Ted Talk.

1. What is a single story?
2. What is an example of a stereotype?
3. Why is the single story dangerous?
4. What is the source of single stories? How are they perpetuated?
5. What is an example of a single story that you have received about other groups?
6. What is an example of a single story that other communities have had about you?
7. What are ways to combat the single story?

References

Delgado, R., & Stefancic, J. (2017). *Critical race theory: An introduction.* New York University Press.

Delpit, L. (2006). *Other people's children: Cultural conflict in the classroom.* The New Press.

DiAngelo, R. (2018). *White fragility: Why it's so hard for white people to talk about racism*. Beacon Press.

Glenn, S.E., & Linton, C. (2005). *Courageous Conversations About Race: A field guide for achieving equity in schools*. Corwin Press.

Hines-Gaither, K. (2015). *Negotiations of race, class, and gender among Afro Latina women immigrants to the southern United States*. https://salemcollege.on.worldcat.org/search?query String=krishauna#/oclc/914234316

Kemp, A. (2016). *Say the wrong thing: Stories and strategies for racial justice and authentic community*. Racial Justice from the H.E.A.R.T. Publishers.

Ladson-Billings, G. (1995). Toward a theory of culturally relevant pedagogy. *American Educational Research Journal*, 32(3), 465–491.

Simmons, D. (2019, October 1). *How to be an antiracist educator*. ASCD. www.ascd.org/el/articles/how-to-be-an-antiracist-educator

Singleton, G.E., & Linton, C. (2005). *Courageous conversations about race: A field guide for achieving equity in schools*. Corwin Press.

4

Designing Antiracist Units of Study

I have witnessed the effects of White supremacy and anti-BIPOC by the entitlement that some feel to access the languages of those who have been marginalized, displaced or whose languages and language practices have been historically belittled.

(Ignacio Carvajal Regidor, Maya K'iche' and other Indigenous languages, University of Kansas)

Framing Documents

In the introduction, we introduced the WRS (The National Standards Collaborative Board, 2015) and the *Six Dimensions of Antiracism in World Languages*. We explained that both frameworks are designed to work synergistically to reach language and proficiency goals. Since the standards are not a curriculum roadmap and only provide general guidance for language learners, we recommend that educators also incorporate other foundational documents. These include, but are not limited to, the NCSSFL-ACTFL *Can-Do Statements* (NCSSFL-ACTFL, 2017), ACTFL

DOI: 10.4324/9781003218265-5

Proficiency Guidelines (2012) and Teaching Tolerance's *Social Justice Standards* (2016). Each document serves a unique purpose.

The WRS are composed of five goal areas. These goals "establish an inextricable link between communication and culture, which is applied in making connections and comparisons and in using this competence to be part of local and global communities" (National Standards Collaborative Board, 2015, para. 1). The NCSSFL-ACTFL *Can-Do Statements* provide self-evaluative proficiency benchmarks that are organized by mode of communication and intercultural communication. The *Can-Do Statements* detail what the learner can produce with the target language. The ACTFL *Proficiency Guidelines* describe what learners can do with the target language based on the four modalities of "speaking, writing, listening, and reading in real-world situations in a spontaneous and non-rehearsed context" (ACTFL *Proficiency Guidelines*, 2012). Teaching Tolerance, now known as Learning for Justice, developed the *Social Justice Standards* (Teaching Tolerance, 2016), the Teaching Tolerance Anti-bias Framework. These standards "are a set of anchor standards and age-appropriate learning outcomes divided into four domains—identity, diversity, justice and action (IDJA)" (p. 3). Finally, consider how your state world language frameworks, standards and benchmarks serve as a foundation for your instructional and language learning goals.

As addressed in the introduction, none of these documents reference race or antiracism. For this reason, we have established the *Six Dimensions of Antiracism in World Languages* as a framing document for antiracist world language classrooms. For the strongest antiracist instructional planning, we believe it is important for educators to seek guidance from multiple framing documents, while intentionally incorporating the missing element of antiracism. A model that supports these frameworks is backward design.

When planning thematic units, educators should consider the elements displayed in the following graphic. As instructors contemplate the **learning outcomes** for the unit, they will consider language proficiency and antiracism outcomes. The antiracist unit will incorporate at least one of the *Six Dimensions of*

Antiracism. When determining how the unit should be assessed, formative assessments should be included so that students receive feedback throughout the unit and can gage their progress and performance. Summative assessments are helpful in bringing the different functions of the unit together. These assessments bring closure and allow the students to see how their learning has progressed over time. The **lesson and unit planning** should build on the students' **schemata**, which represent their prior knowledge. It is important to understand that students enter our classrooms with a foundation on which to build, and not as blank slates. The goal of the unit is to simultaneously raise our students' antiracist consciousness and also their language proficiency.

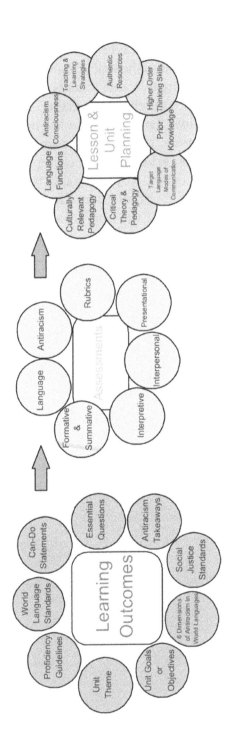

What is Backward Design?

Backward design (also known as understanding by design) is a method for setting the goals you would like to achieve before determining instructional goals and assessments. This framework was designed by Jay McTighe and Grant Wiggins. It is termed "backward" because you are working from the rear. This is different from a traditional lesson plan in which educators may begin with activities and end with the assessment. In *Understanding by design*, McTighe & Wiggins (2012) argue that backward design reroutes the focus from the teacher to the learner. With a goal-oriented approach, educators are forced to consider how the lesson or unit will meet the needs of the learners. This approach places the activities in the background, and the desired results in the foreground. Backward design also aligns well with our introductory query of *what's your why*. Having to reflect on the rationale, motivations and purpose will enable us to approach our work in a more meaningful and thoughtful manner.

The backward design framework illustrates the ways in which we should envision our role in the classroom as **teacher-facilitators**. As such, we are coaching our students and they sit at the center of our instruction. We are providing opportunities for our students to build on their **existing critical thinking skills**. We believe that our students possess these skills, and we seek to build upon that foundation. We encourage higher order thinking not by telling our students how to think or what to think, but rather we assist them in their thinking process through metacognitive inquiry. According to Metcalfe and Shimamura (1994), **metacognition** is a consciousness of one's own thought processes and an understanding of the unique patterns that influence our thoughts. In other words, why do we think the way that we do? Some ways of promoting metacognition include reflective exercises, silence practices, meditation exercises and social-emotional intelligence lessons, etc. Backward design offers a framework to develop our unit and lesson plans. We begin with the lesson goals in mind, and in doing so we increase our students' capacity to gain these essential skills. Using backward design helps to dismantle superficial treatment of the language classroom.

Three Stages of Backward Design

The backward design model is composed of three stages: 1) iden-tify desired results; 2) determine acceptable evidence; 3) plan learning experiences and instruction. We will discuss each stage below, and present essential questions to ground each stage. We will also frame backward design in the context of the antiracist world language classroom.

Stage 1: Identify Desired Results

Stage 1 is an opportunity for educators to consider the big pic-ture and the end game. Educators should ask themselves the fol-lowing questions as they seek to identify the desired outcomes of their antiracist lessons or units of study.

Ask Yourself!

◆ With what language and antiracist content, informa-tion and perspectives should students engage in order to increase their understanding?
◆ What language and antiracist knowledge and capaci-ties should students build during the unit?
◆ What key language and antiracist points and take-aways should students retain beyond the course completion?

Stage 2: Determine Acceptable Evidence

In the second stage of the backward design model, educators should consider which language modalities (interpretive, inter-personal, presentational) students will access, and how their performance will be assessed. The goal of stage two is to receive evidence that students have retained the information and built the desired capacities.

Ask Yourself!

◆ What is acceptable evidence of students' language proficiency and antiracist awareness?
◆ How will I confirm that the students have achieved the desired language and antiracist results?
◆ How do my assessments align with the goals of stage one?

Common Language Assessments

◆ discussion questions;
◆ oral proficiency interviews;
◆ short-answer quizzes;
◆ free-response questions;
◆ homework assignments;
◆ listening/auditory assignments;
◆ speaking/oral assignments;
◆ role play and skits;
◆ interpretive, interpersonal and presentational tasks;
◆ and many more.

Antiracist Assessments

◆ discussion questions;
◆ analyzing topics from multiple perspectives including BIPOC;
◆ asking and answering queries related to race;
◆ activities related to intersectionality;
◆ reflective exercises;
◆ social identity-based exercises;
◆ assessments of power, privilege and oppression;
◆ connecting how racialized history informs today's legacies;

◆ connecting how colonization, settler colonialism and imperialism and other forms of domination inform today's legacies;
◆ creating and engaging with counter stories;
◆ drafting public service announcements on antiracism;
◆ composing a 140-character twitter post on antiracism;
◆ incorporating family–school–community engagements via interviews or service learning, etc.;
◆ and many more.

Stage 3: Plan Learning Experiences and Instruction

The final stage of backward design is for educators to map out how they will teach the lesson or unit. At this stage, the educator outlines the language and antiracist instructional strategies and activities. As in the assessment stage, the learning experiences and instruction should have alignment with the overall goals of the lesson or unit.

Ask Yourself!

◆ What background knowledge (content, perspectives, data, facts) and skills (intergroup dialogue, communication, problem solving, listening) will students need in order to achieve language and antiracism goals?
◆ What activities will maximize students' knowledge and skill-building?
◆ What will need to be shared, taught and facilitated and how should it be accomplished to achieve language and antiracism goals?
◆ What materials, resources and perspectives are needed to realize proficiency and antiracism goals?

In an antiracist world language classroom, educators must consider which **instructional strategies** best align with an antiracist classroom. Many of the strategies and assessments already utilized in world language classrooms will work well for the antiracist classroom. Almost any plan of instruction that helps the student to learn the language or to negotiate the language learning process can be considered an instructional strategy (Shrum and Glisan, 2005). What adds value to antiracist instruction is explicitly educating and/or celebrating race or ethnicity while interrogating colorism and racism and promoting antiracism as an instructional goal or dimension. Some instructional strategies that can facilitate both language and antiracism goals follow:

- flipped classroom
- incorporating technologies such as Mote, Slidemania, Loom, etc.
- speaker-listener-observer
- large and/or small group discussions
- intergroup dialogue
- student-led facilitation
- roleplay
- interviewing community members with unique experiences and perspectives
- theatre of the oppressed activities (such as leaving a roleplay unresolved and allowing audience to help to resolve the situation)
- observation

Since backward design was not created specifically for world languages, we would like to address some of the benefits and challenges of the model. We feel backward design is a useful model in that it calls for higher level thinking from the lesson's inception. The model goes from whole to parts and lends well to a scaffolded approach in world languages. That said, backward design also exposes certain challenges. Review the proceeding list of pros and cons and consider what else might you add. Following the list, we will address each challenge by offering considerations and classroom examples of how educators might address those challenges.

Benefits of Backward Design	Challenges of Backward Design
◆ Student-focused	◆ Must reach both language and antiracism goals
◆ Offers the big picture	◆ Antiracism goals may not be textbook-driven, requiring outside resources
◆ Purpose-driven	◆ Students who are used to activity-focused instruction (*the what*) will have to shift their practice in order to first consider *the why*
◆ Requires more thoughtful engagement, and less focus on *doing* and *busyness*	◆ Although students can develop these skills, they may not initially have the language resources or maturity needed to speak on higher level topics

Challenges of Backward Design	Responses to the Challenges	Examples
◆ Must reach both language and antiracism goals	◆ Do not view language and antiracism goals as mutually exclusive. Consider intertextuality. How can language goals also be informed by antiracism goals?	German professor Priscilla Layne incorporates excerpts of May Ayim's poem, *Autumn in Germany*. Ayim's poem is about racist violence in Germany. But Ayim uses a specific aesthetic approach to get her point across, like writing in all lower case, using repetition and ambiguous language.
◆ Antiracism goals may not be textbook-driven, requiring outside resources	◆ The initial research to design antiracist lessons may take time, but once created they can be recycled from year to year. ◆ Consider how students can support your research so that they share the responsibility for creating an antiracist classroom.	View the web companion site for this book (www.routledge.com/9781032065694). Spanish teacher Richard de Meij has compiled a wealth of antiracist resources that can be incorporated into your language classroom (https://docs.google.com/document/d/1nkhY7IJZwTbtbaQPESoy0im6lITdBhCM6fZmdAUahsI/edit?usp=sharing) .

Challenges of Backward Design	Responses to the Challenges	Examples
	◆ Collaborate with colleagues both within the language department and in other disciplines to share ideas and create a repertoire of antiracist resources. ◆ Avail yourself to the resources available online and through professional conference presentations and workshops.	
◆ Students who are used to activity-focused instruction (*the what*) will have to shift their practice in order to first consider *the why*.	◆ Early in the term, ask students their goals for taking your course. Be open to a variety of responses, even if they do not align with your instructional or course goals. Use the information to better serve your students and to enhance your practice.	◆ Use jamboard or your whiteboard to share your daily goals, lessons or unit goals with students. ◆ See jamboard activity in the following section. ◆ Consider ways that you can co-construct lessons and unit goals with students (see section Combating Overplanning).
	◆ Oftentimes lesson plans are only seen by instructors and administration. Although students may not need to see the entire lesson plan, show them your goals for each unit or lesson and the essential questions. This	

Challenges of Backward Design	Responses to the Challenges	Examples
	will enable them to know where you will end up from the beginning, and give them direction for the day or week. Sharing this content will also enable students to consider their roles and responsibilities in the lesson.	
◆ Although students can develop these skills, they may not initially have the language resources or maturity needed to speak on higher level topics.	◆ Students should have the opportunity to engage in antiracist units or lessons at all levels of instruction. ◆ Oftentimes immaturity is due to a lack of exposure to certain content, disinterest, discomfort, or a lack of trust built within the language learning community.	**Limited linguistic resources** ◆ Scaffold your lessons so that there are multiple entry points. ◆ View the proficiency checks throughout this text to serve as a guide for how to adjust your lessons to the novice level and beyond.
		Trust-Building ◆ Have a positive first touch by meeting individually with each student in person or using technology. This can occur over the summer or winter break or in individual meetings with students once school has begun. These are short meetings where the instructors introduce themselves to students and get to know them.

Challenges of Backward Design	Responses to the Challenges	Examples
		Then, the language and antiracism goals are incorporated into the conversation. Be sure to allow space for students to share, and not just for the instructor to talk *at* the student. ◆ In line with culturally responsive pedagogy, learn how the students, their families and communities add value to the language classroom. 　◆ Students can keep journals of when/where they hear languages spoken in their communities. 　◆ Offer extra credit if you run into students outside of school and they speak to you or to their peers in the target language. **Note:** Encouraging students to speak to peers builds community. Also, broadening out-of-school communication beyond the instructor is a good way to not unfairly advantage students who may have more access to the instructor based on residence and social class.

Building Trust into Unit Design

Students are more apt to engage in antiracist units of study, see their value and be more open if they feel they can trust the classroom space and those who inhabit it. Educators should plan community-building activities into their units of study. Focusing on antiracist content with no attention to creating a conducive and equitable space leaves a major gap in instruction, and opens the door to challenges down the road. To establish a rapport with students from the beginning, ask them to create a jamboard with the following content. This outcome can also be accomplished by responding to the same questions on an index card. Teachers can also use the responses to the jamboard as the basis for individualized meetings with students.

Students have created their jamboards, you have held individualized meetings and now it is time to get up and get moving. Teachers can use the questions above about interests outside of school to engage students in a meet and greet activity. The teacher creates a diversity bingo sheet that has different interests and information that the teacher has learned from the students' jamboards or other conversations. Students stand up and navigate the classroom to introduce themselves and to meet their peers. In the target language, they ask "who is an only child." They use the target language to place as many of their classmates' names in the boxes as possible. They are timed, and the student with the most boxes filled wins a prize from your prize box. This is a great activity to build community, to learn names and to use the target language at the novice level.

To teach you I must know you.
Meet & Greet: Quién...; Qui...

Es la/el mayor de la familia Oldest of the family Est l'aíné de la famille	Es hija/o única/o Only child Est enfant unique	Es de primer año Freshman Dans sa première année à L'université	Es de Virginia Is from Virginia Est de Virginie	Tiene 18 años Is 18 years old A 18 ans
Tiene 4–5 hermanas/os Has 4–5 siblings A 4–5 frères et soeurs	Trabaja en el centro comercial Works at the mall Travaille dans un centre commercial/centre d'achats	Es la/el menor de la familia Youngest of the family Est la/le benjamin/e de la famille	Va a la iglesia regularmente Goes to church regularly Va à l'églìse régulièrement	Toca un instrumento musical Plays instrument Joue un instrument musical
Está en un conjunto musical/coro In a band Est dans un orchestre ou dans une chorale	Trabaja en un restaurante Works in a restaurant Travaille dans un restaurant	Es de tercer año Is a junior Est dans sa troisième année à L'université	Le gustan las matemáticas Likes math Aime les mathématiques	Juega un deporte Plays a sport Joue au sport
Quiere ser maestra/o Wants to be a teacher Veut être une/un enseignante/enseignant	Baila muy bien Dances well Danse très bien	Canta muy bien Sings well Chante très bien	Va a la discoteca regularmente Goes to dance clubs regularly Va à la discothèque régulièrement	Tiene novia/o Has a girlfriend/boyfriend A une petite copine/un petit copain

Planning the Unit

As you plan the unit of study, first consider the overall **theme** of the unit. What is the key concept or focus of the unit? Any good research study begins with questions for inquiry. For example, what do you hope to learn, find out, or study? Therefore, determine the essential questions. These questions are the framing points of inquiry of study. **Essential questions** should be open ended so that they evoke curiosity and thoughtful responses. Next, determine the antiracism takeaway. The **antiracism takeaway** is typically a definitive statement or declaration that serves as a statement of understanding. This statement grounds the unit and illustrates the key point, fact or idea that is to be recalled.

Next, the **goals** outline what a learner will be able to do upon completion of the unit. Goals might also be called unit objectives. We recommend a reflection of the unit goals before determining the **WRS**. The WRS or other framing documents, as listed previously, will enable the planner to focus on language learning outcomes. The previous points of engagement (themes, essential questions, antiracism takeaways and goals) should drive the standards and not the reverse. Knowing your goals will assist you to frame the lesson or unit properly within the WRS. In other words, what language resources need to be accessed in order to reach the goals of the unit? Note, you may also elect to use a different framework (i.e., *Can-Do Statements*, etc.) or different standards other than the WRS if they are more appropriate for your lesson.

Next, all antiracism units and lessons should include a component of the *Six Dimensions of Antiracism in World Languages*. Review each of the six dimensions to determine which best align with your unit objectives. Then decide how you will measure if your lesson goals have been achieved. This reflection will determine your assessment aims. Finally, the activities that you select should reinforce all aspects of the unit plan from the theme to the assessments.

Ask Yourself!

◆ What do my students need to *do* (activities) to be able to accomplish the goals of the unit? As you are crafting your unit, outline the series of lessons that you will include to reach the unit goals.

Glynn et al (2018) explained, "The unit goals must reflect a variety of lower-order and higher order thinking skills; to succeed in the unit, students will need to engage in a range of thinking and skills" (p. 36). Reflect on how your language and antiracism goals align, as well as how those goals support your students' existing critical thinking and awareness, and build upon that foundation. Now you see how the backward design model breaks from traditional lesson planning structures by beginning with the big picture, and then working its way toward the activities needed to reach the unit goals. Following are questions for consideration and reflection that will aid you in planning your unit of study.

Ask Yourself!

◆ What is driving my unit of study (current events, personal interests, interests of students, popular culture, etc.)?
◆ How are the language goals supporting the antiracism goals and vice versa?
◆ Who or what do I need to assist me in reaching my unit objectives?
◆ What is the current proficiency level of the students (novice, intermediate, advanced, etc.)?
◆ How can students demonstrate proficiency in the modes of communication (presentational, interpretative, interpersonal)?

As teachers reflect on their unit and lesson planning goals, they might consider the following questions posed by McTighe and Wiggins (2012, p. 102):

◆ Does the learning plan make clear to students where they're going (the learning goals), why (reason for learning the content) and what is required of them (performance requirements and evaluative criteria)?
◆ Does the learning plan include one or more hooks to engage learners around the unit's important ideas?
◆ Does the learning plan provide adequate opportunities for students to explore big ideas and essential questions, and to receive instruction to equip them for the required performance?
◆ Does the learning plan provide sufficient opportunities for learners to rethink, rehearse, revise, or refine their work based upon timely feedback?
◆ Does the learning plan include opportunities for students to self-evaluate their work, reflect on their learning and set future goals?

Reflections by Students

In order for students to self-evaluate their work and unit experience, it is important to incorporate reflective exercises. We referenced metacognition earlier in this chapter. Both the learner and the educator should reflect on the unit before it is implemented, as it is underway and after its implementation. Depending upon the class dynamic, size, etc., the teacher may ask students to write down their reflections on a lesson or unit plan. Students can complete the reflection openly or anonymously. Then the teacher may collect their reflections and use them as feedback for enhancing their unit of study or future units, or they may evoke a class discussion related to the current unit.

Students' Reflections on Unit of Study

Introducing the Unit

Years ago, we watched commentary from television personality and author Tavis Smiley. He was speaking candidly on his talk show, which bore the author's name. Smiley spoke about the need to include antiracism in our academic programs. He served an indictment on education by probing the sequences of our lessons. Smiley questioned why educators often begin their antiracism lessons with the colonized lands and settler colonialists (see Chapter 2). He encouraged educators to begin antiracism units by incorporating the histories of oppressed people before they were colonized. To that end we might consider, what is the history of African nations prior to European colonization? What is the history and lived experiences of Indigenous people prior to settler colonialism? How did these communities and many others live and govern themselves prior to external domination?

Whatever the starting point may be, educators need to give thoughtful attention to and articulate why they choose to start at a certain location or entry point. What is the rationale? What is gained? What is lost? The starting point is the learners' first touch with your unit of study. Consider this. When you meet someone for the first time, that first impression is lasting and often shapes your future exchanges and perceptions. The unit of study is no different. Take time to cultivate a relationship between your students and the unit. This cultivation can be done through the community-building activities presented through-out this book or by ensuring that there is a proper introduction to your unit. Take time to get this right. Even consider practicing your delivery and introduction of the unit before implementing it. You might also share your unit with a colleague for feedback.

In addition to determining the starting point of your unit, think about the theme, goals, essential questions and key take-aways of the unit. Use that understanding to incorporate the daily lessons that are needed to meet your overall goals and objectives. All lessons, or roads, within the unit should lead back to the theme.

Combating Overplanning

Recently, I (Krishauna) was teaching a course on antiracist edu-cation. I inadvertently omitted a date from the syllabus. Prior to the omitted date, the class was working on a unit of study on environmentalism. Specifically, we were studying the nuclear chemical testing that had been done on the Marshall Islands by the United States and its lasting negative impact. According to a report published by the *Los Angeles Times*, "Between 1946 and 1958, the United States detonated 67 nuclear bombs on, in and above the Marshall Islands — vaporizing whole islands, carving craters into its shallow lagoons and exiling hundreds of people from their homes" (Rust, 2019, para. 3). My students were very engaged in this topic and immediately made connections to similar injustices that occurred in Puerto Rico (Agent Orange) and other parts of the world.

Due to my faux pas of omitting a date from the syllabus, in essence, we had a free day. Instead of trying to fill the time haphazardly, I asked each student (about 11) to share information with the class on the topic of environmentalism or environmental justice. They could select any topic that was meaningful to them. Students shared about pollution in their countries of origin or their hometowns. They shared about the coffee industry and unethical sourcing. They shared about the large quantities of waste and chemicals used by clothing manufacturers. They shared podcasts such as *Living Downstream* which is committed to environmental justice. They shared information on environmental artists such as Robert Morris and environmentally conscious musicians such as Childish Gambino and his song, *Feels like Summer*. Students educated their peers and me on information with which many of us were unfamiliar. Seeing my enthusiasm for what they shared, a student even gifted me with the book, *Emergent Strategy: Shaping change, changing minds* by Adrienne Maree Brown. This unplanned serendipitous class was one of the highlights of the term, and by far one of the most informative.

Ask Yourself!

◆ Is it possible that we are overplanning?
◆ Is there flexibility in your curricular design or is each instructional day already pre-planned?
◆ How can students assume a more active role in the production of knowledge?

To this end, McTighe and Wiggins (2012) concluded,

> Try to build in at least one day in your unit plan when noth-
> ing is planned. Because adjustments are inevitable (based
> on results of formative assessments), you have to "design
> in" time to adjust. In other words, the best designs are not
> overpacked and set in stone but are modifiable and adjusted
> as needed to cause the desired results. You have to plan to
> adjust. At the very least, that means not overplanning and
> then convincing yourself that there is no time to adjust.
>
> (p. 102)

Following, you will find two units of study that incorporate the
instructional design elements that we have highlighted throughout this book and in this chapter.

Ask Yourself!

◆ How might you adapt these units for your antiracist
world language classroom?

ANTIRACIST WORLD LANGUAGE LESSON TEMPLATE	
Instructor	Alice Miano, Spanish, Stanford University
Language	Applicable to all languages, some Spanish resources
Language level	Scaffolded for Novice to Intermediate
Unit Theme (Include the key, central and/or overarching focus of the lesson or unit.)	**Indigenous Peoples at Home and Abroad** A unit on Indigenous peoples could focus on land, language and cultural maintenance rights, comparing situations and contexts at home and abroad. This lesson focuses on land rights in the U.S. and abroad.
Lesson Theme	**Seeing Indigenous peoples through land acknowledgements**

ANTIRACIST WORLD LANGUAGE LESSON TEMPLATE	
Essential Question(s) (Pose questions that may require more than one lesson, are open-ended, stimulate thought and spark curiosity, concern or inquiry.)	◆ What does it mean to be Indigenous? ◆ Who are the Indigenous peoples who populate the area where we live and/or attend school? ◆ Who are the Indigenous peoples who populate one or more of our target language regions? (The instructor may wish to limit the whole class to the study of one target language region or country, or to one Indigenous group, or to allow students (individually or collectively) to choose an Indigenous group to study.) ◆ What is their history? What are their present-day circumstances and concerns, both at home and in the target language region(s) we are studying? ◆ How can students be effective allies at home and abroad?
Antiracism Takeaway (Key antiracism perspective, understanding or focus)	Despite past injustices, including human and cultural genocide as well as the theft of lands, the Indigenous continue to live in vibrant communities and to seek justice for themselves and others. Many still struggle to gain land rights to territories lost over the centuries and continuously today.
Lesson Objectives and Goals (Upon completion, students will be able to…)	◆ Articulate characteristics of Indigenous heritage ◆ Identify Native inhabitants of certain regions ◆ Compare historical events to contemporary circumstances ◆ Examine the skills needed for effective allyship
World Readiness Standards (Include one or more of the *World Readiness Standards* into the lesson or unit plan.)	◆ Interpersonal exchanges. ◆ Interpretive listening (and reading) of authentic materials. ◆ Presentational language through land acknowledgements and debate.
Linguistic Functions (language targets focus, and linguistic goals and functions of the unit or lesson)	◆ Formulating questions. ◆ Past and present narration and description. ◆ Expressing opinions. ◆ Present and past tense verbs. Connective phrases. ◆ Descriptive vocabulary related to land and rights.

ANTIRACIST WORLD LANGUAGE LESSON TEMPLATE	
Six Dimensions of Antiracism in World Languages (Include one or more of the *Six Dimensions of Antiracism in World Languages* into the lesson or unit plan.)	**6. SYSTEMIC/STRUCTURAL/ HISTORICAL:** Focus on historical and systematic operations and legacies ◆ Examine the historical roots and contemporary manifestations of racial prejudice and discrimination. ◆ Explore the role that history, government, geopolitics, colonialism, imperialism, settler colonialism and the like have on education and systemic racism.
Assessments (Include summative or formative assessment delineated by communicative, interpretive and/or presentational modes.)	**Presentational:** Students draft original land acknowledgement statements in the target language (Intermediate or above) or in English (Novice) through process writing which may include multiple drafts.
Activities (Include activities, tasks and engagements that serve to reach the lesson goals, objectives and/or respond to the essential question(s).)	**Initial pre-lesson brainstorming:** ◆ "Tomorrow we'll be learning about Indigenous communities in… [target language region]. But first, what Indigenous communities inhabit our local lands?" ◆ Teacher presents concepts from United Nations handout (available here and under "Resources" below) to help students conceptualize the definition of "Indigenous peoples." ◆ Students then brainstorm about who local Indigenous peoples are (whether local to home, school, or both if different) at the instructor's discretion. A great tool to begin identifying Native lands is https://native-land.ca to find the names of local Indigenous groups. ◆ If little is known about Indigenous communities, then that is a point to note! Many U.S. history textbooks currently used offer little specific information about Indigenous peoples. Students may want to question why that is so.

ANTIRACIST WORLD LANGUAGE LESSON TEMPLATE	
	Teacher Input Phase: Day 1 ◆ Students return to class and share information. Teacher organizes students into sharing groups. Students with Intermediate level oral proficiency (or higher) can share in the target language. Novice level students would need to share in the school language. ◆ **Target language input:** Teacher presents material in the target language to further draw students into the topic. **Student Output Phase: Day 2** ◆ **Land acknowledgements:** Consulting from among the websites listed below under "Resources" as well as the accompanying handout and other resources, the teacher presents the idea of land acknowledgements. **Student Output Phase: Day 3** ◆ Students present their land acknowledgements. ◆ As a final step, students rehearse and present their land acknowledgements to the class in the coming days. These presentations can be assessed based on the verifiability of information presented, social appropriateness and oral delivery. ◆ Students may wish to consider presenting their rehearsed, polished land acknowledgments at a formal event on campus.

ANTIRACIST WORLD LANGUAGE LESSON TEMPLATE	

Resources (web and print resources to accompany or referenced in the unit)	◆ **Book:** Andrés Reséndez. *The Other Slavery: The Uncovered Story of Indian Enslavement in America.*
	 ◆ **Museum:** National Museum of the American Indian: https://americanindian.si.edu
	 ◆ **Podcast:** "Repairing the Past: Returning Native Land" (an episode of the *Be Antiracist* podcast). Includes several additional resources: https://tinyurl.com/mr2v65u7
	 ◆ **Spanish Language Resources: Juan Carlos** Espinosa. "Encarcelados por no hablar español: la agonía de los indígenas en las prisiones en México". *El País.* July 15, 2021: https://tinyurl.com/wz9wj5w6
	 ◆ **Land rights and governance:**
	   ◆ **In English:** Indian Law Resource Center. Land Rights: https://indianlaw.org/issue/land-rights
	   ◆ **In Spanish:** Artículo 26. Declaración de las Naciones Unidas sobre los derechos de los pueblos indígenas: https://tinyurl.com/52ph2m23
	 ◆ **Allyship/Advocacy**
	   ◆ The Warrior Women Project: www.warriorwomen.org

ANTIRACIST WORLD LANGUAGE LESSON TEMPLATE	
Instructor	Nodia Mena, University of North Carolina at Greensboro
Language	Garífuna and Spanish
Language level	Intermediate Low
Unit Theme (Include the key, central and/or overarching focus of the lesson or unit.)	Black Garífuna Past and Present
Essential Question(s) (Pose questions that may require more than one lesson, are open-ended, stimulate thought and spark curiosity, concern or inquiry.)	◆ Who are the Garífuna people group? ◆ What is the history of the Garífuna? ◆ What are their experiences today? ◆ What cultural products and perspectives have survived?

ANTIRACIST WORLD LANGUAGE LESSON TEMPLATE	
Antiracism Takeaway (Key antiracism perspective, understanding or focus)	Although Black Garífuna have been in Central America since the 18th century, they are still treated as strangers in their own land.
Lesson Objectives and Goals (Upon completion, students will be able to…)	◆ Describe moments in the history of the Garífuna people and evaluate their significance, especially their connection to the modern world. ◆ Analyze corporal and oral forms of communication among the Garífuna. ◆ Compare the lived experience of the Garífuna to the current public discourse. ◆ Participate in a demonstration of Garífuna traditions.
World Readiness Standards (Include one or more of the *World Readiness Standards* into the lesson or unit plan.)	◆ **Culture:** Interact with cultural understanding ◆ **Relating Cultural Practices to Perspectives:** Learners use the language to investigate, explain and reflect on the relationship between the practices and perspectives of the cultures studied. ◆ **Relating Cultural Products to Perspectives:** Learners use the language to investigate, explain and reflect on the relationship between the products and perspectives of the cultures studied. ◆ **Interpretive Communication:** Learners understand, interpret and analyze what is heard, read, or viewed on a variety of topics. ◆ **Presentational Communication:** Learners present information, concepts and ideas to inform, explain, persuade and narrate on a variety of topics using appropriate media and adapting to various audiences of listeners, readers, or viewers.

ANTIRACIST WORLD LANGUAGE LESSON TEMPLATE	
Linguistic Functions (language targets focus, and linguistic goals and functions of the unit or lesson)	◆ Focus on interpreting texts in Garífuna and Spanish. ◆ Focus on listening comprehension in Spanish.
Six Dimensions of Antiracism in World Languages (Include one or more of the *Six Dimensions of Antiracism in World Languages* into the lesson or unit plan.)	◆ **Interpersonal:** Address how race, ethnicity, racism, antiracism, colorism and other forms of oppression operate on an interpersonal level. ◆ **Interpersonal:** Discuss how race intersects with other identities such as ethnicity, class, gender, sexuality, religion, environmentalism, immigration status, documentation, disability, etc. ◆ **Cultural/Societal:** Address how race, ethnicity, racism, antiracism, colorism and other forms of oppression operate on cultural and societal levels. ◆ **Cultural/Societal:** Incorporate diverse populations, diverse experiences and diverse cultures of the target language. ◆ **Curricular/Classroom/ Department:** Present diverse perspectives, representations and counter stories/ counternarratives.
Assessments (Include summative or formative assessment delineated by communicative, interpretive and/or presentational modes.)	◆ Students will take a written exam upon completion of the unit. ◆ Students will present Garífuna movements and dances, and explain the history surrounding them in Spanish.
Unit Design (Include activities, tasks and engagements that serve to reach the lesson goals, objectives and/or respond to the essential question(s).)	

ANTIRACIST WORLD LANGUAGE LESSON TEMPLATE		
Week 1	**Introduction/Overview**	**Reading:** Gates, Jr., *Black in Latin America*; Mena and Ali, "Garífunas in the African Diaspora," pp. 1- 4 **Reading:** Taylor, *The Black Carib Wars: Freedom, Survival, and the Making of the Garífuna*, Ch. 1; Ch. 2; Terminología; Terminologie Yellow Carib (Arawak, Kallínagu) Black Carib Garífuna (Garinagu) Ladinos (White, light Guatemalans) Yurumein (St. Vincent & Grenadines)
Week 2	**Separation from Saint Vincent**	Discuss the exile of the Garífuna by the British, and wars with Spain and France. These conflicts led to the forced exile of almost 5,000 Garífuna to Central America. Answer the following questions. ◆ **Where were they sent after Balliceaux?** ◆ After being sent to Balliceaux and living there for about a year, all remaining Garífuna were sent to Roatan, off the coast of Honduras, by the British. Today, Garífuna groups live in Honduras, Guatemala, Latin America, Belize, Nicaragua, St. Vincent and many other places. ◆ **Possible consequences (psychological, social)** ◆ As a result of this forced removal, the Garífuna most likely experienced trauma both personally and in their identity as a group. Forced removal is a huge source of trauma stress for individuals, and can contribute to an increase in chronic disease and other health outcomes. Socially, it is surprising that Garífuna identity has remained so strongly intact for so long. Many times, forced removal causes a fragmentation in group identity, resulting in a creation of separate ethnic groups entirely.

ANTIRACIST WORLD LANGUAGE LESSON TEMPLATE		
Week 3	**Identity**	◆ Watch this video (https://tinyurl.com/2p8k84zc) that highlights that Garífuna people of Latin America tend to feel more connected to Garífuna of other countries, than to White or lighter skinned Latin Americans in their own country. ◆ Watch this YouTube clip (https://tinyurl.com/yu7fpa74) that highlights the discrimination experienced by Garífuna people.
Week 5	**Culture**	Listen to this traditional Garífuna song about singers trying to affirm that they have good intentions. What do you notice about the Garífuna words? ◆ Mama wualujaña uribanai ya (We are not looking for trouble.) ◆ Wasaniajaruguña (We are just having a good time.) ◆ Mama walujaña uribani ya ◆ Wasaniajaruguña ◆ Saraba ye, saraba ye (Wake up now, wake up now.) ◆ Daraba-y bubenary hun parandatiñun (Open the door to us, the singers.) Watch this video (www.youtube.com/watch?v=TdFr_mLSqa0) to learn the traditional Garífuna dance and its meaning. Video depicts **Hamalali Wayunagu** (Name of the Theatrical Dance Group) Watch this video (https://youtu.be/JwxGBcaOqnA) to learn Wanaragua, a dance performed by men in colonial times to protect Garífuna women against sexual assault from the Spaniards. Wanaragua: Dance Ritual Coropatia: Theater

ANTIRACIST WORLD LANGUAGE LESSON TEMPLATE		
Week 5	**Presentations**	Understanding the meaning of the dance, students will work in groups to practice movements associated with the dance, and then present the movements to the class. During the presentations, students will describe the meaning of the dances in Spanish.
	Resources (web and print resources to accompany or referenced in the unit)	◆ *Sojourners of the Caribbean: Ethnogenesis and Ethnohistory of the Garífuna*, pp. 171–193 ◆ *Disparate Diasporas: Identity and Politics in an African-Nicaraguan Community*, pp. 33–50 ◆ Tayac, *IndiVisible: African-Native American Lives in the Americas*, pp. 35–57 and 91–117 ◆ De la Fuente and Andrews, *Afro-Latin American Studies*, pp. 348–395

References

American Council on the Teaching of Foreign Languages (ACTFL). (2012). *ACTFL proficiency guidelines 2012.* www.actfl.org/sites/default/files/guidelines/ACTFL ProficiencyGuidelines2012.pdf

Glynn, C., Wesely, P., Wassell, B. (2018). *Words and actions: Teaching languages through the lens of social justice* (2nd ed.). The American Council on the Teaching of Foreign Languages.

Metcalfe, J., & Shimamura, A.P. (Eds.). (1994). *Metacognition: Knowing about knowing.* The MIT Press. https://doi.org/10.7551/mitpress/4561.001.0001

National Council of State Supervisors for Languages-American Council on the Teaching of Foreign Languages (NCSSFL-ACTFL). (2017). *NCSSFL-ACTFL can-do-statements.* American Council on the Teaching of Foreign Languages. www.actfl.org/sites/default/files/can-dos/Can-Do_Benchmarks_Indicators.pdf

National Standards Collaborative Board. (2015). *World-Readiness Standards for Learning Languages* (4th ed.). www.actfl.org/resources/world-readiness-standards-learning-languages

Rust, S. (2019, November 10). How the U.S. betrayed the Marshall Islands, kindling the next nuclear disaster. *Los AngelesTimes*.www.latimes.com/projects/marshall-islands-nuclear-testing-sea-level-rise/

Shrum, J.L., & Glisan, E.W. (2005). *Teacher's handbook: Contextualized language instruction* (3rd ed.). Thomson Heinle.

Teaching Tolerance. (2016). *Social justice standards: The teaching tolerance anti-bias framework.* www.learningforjustice.org/sites/default/files/2017-06/TT_Social_Justice_Standards_0.pdf

Wiggins, G. & McTighe, J. (2012). *Understanding by design guide to advanced concepts in creating and reviewing units.* Association for Supervision & Curriculum Development.

5

Planning Daily Lessons
on Antiracism

I address important topics through songs: I create a space for my students to discuss important issues without imposing my opinions. I sometimes have to create guided questions to lead the conversations in a certain direction.

(Carine Terras, French, Whitfield School)

Daily lessons are instructional outlines of focused content that are meant for one course period. In practice, a daily lesson may span the course of a few days, but the focus and scope are centered on one aspect of a larger design or unit. In contrast, a unit of study is a systematic approach that incorporates contextualized lessons over time. In a **proficiency-oriented classroom** (see Chapter 7), educators should consider which proficiency outcomes to target. Daily lessons, like units of study, should have both proficiency and antiracist aims. Not every daily lesson will include both paradigms, but it is important to have regular proficiency and antiracist outcomes throughout the lesson plan sequence. Many teachers initially plan their lessons informally by "assessing what their students already know to bring to the learning task and then figuring out what they need to teach them

DOI: 10.4324/9781003218265-6

to get them to the appropriate objective" (Shrum & Glisan, 2005, p. 85).

The **backward design model** presented in Chapter 4 is also a useful tool for daily lesson plans. In keeping with this model, educators will consider the end goal when planning daily lessons. They will contemplate what they want learners to take away from the lesson. Next, they will determine what evidence is needed to assess the learning outcomes. Finally, educators will plan the lesson activities to support their learning goals.

Consider how you will draw students into the classroom space even before the lesson begins. The first few minutes of class is the optimal time for setting the stage. Building on the University of Michigan's framework for intergroup dialogue, consider how you will **build community** during your daily lessons. Here are some options for class-time starters. Middle school Spanish teacher, Laura Boyd, builds community and sets the stage by having a daily warmup with her students. Her warmup only takes about five minutes. Laura (Boyd, 2021, para 2) stated:

> I usually have five review questions from the previous class. During this quick activity, I open the Zoom classroom, and also greet kids at the door of my classroom. All students, regardless of whether they're learning at home or at school, are engaged and getting ready for the day together.

Laura's example is a good way to bridge the previous class with the next daily lesson. In addition to bellringer activities to get students actively engaged and on task within the first few minutes of class, we recommend centering practices for the antiracist classroom.

A **centering practice** is particularly important in an antiracist classroom. Chinese history professor, Zhihong Chen, starts her day with a collective **moment of silence**. In that time, students are invited to de-stress, meditate, pray, or just clear their minds in order to focus on the day ahead and to be present in the space. Education professor, Kimberly Nao, who is African American and Japanese, incorporates **breathing exercises** into her classroom in order to offer students tools to de-compress and to ground themselves in the space. Another option for opening your classroom is to **play music**. Spanish teacher, Jenniffer Whyte, incorporates Latin dance and zumba into her classroom for kinesthetic engagement and to get her students' blood flowing. There are many options that educators can pull from to bring social emotional practice into the language classroom. Christen Campbell stated:

> There is a huge connection to develop students' Social Emotional Learning (SEL) and wellness before engaging in conversations around race. In my class, we do a daily activity around SEL, which helps us grow, develop empathy and create space for understanding of our differences. By setting SEL and engaging in SEL strategies as a foundation, students are more willing to engage in difficult conversations, share their personal experiences and listen empathetically to others.
> (personal communication, June 30, 2021)

We recommend offering multiple practices based on mode of learning and developmental appropriateness. Educators can incorporate these practices throughout the semester or year so that students can be exposed to different options. These practices can also be helpful to diffuse situations when hot moments occur (see Chapter 6).

Opening and Closing with Positivity

Because of the sensitivity of some topics and possible resistance to them, centering practices can be highly effective in the antiracist classroom and create a space for open mindedness. We recommend starting the class with a positive, unifying message, and closing the class in a unifying manner as well. Educators should not confuse opening and closing with positivity as a rationale for not dealing with critical topics. Of course, every lesson may not be appropriate for this structure or lend itself to this design.

Positivity does not shield the antiracist classroom from challenging topics, but rather they set the atmosphere for these discussions to happen more earnestly. You might open and close the class by considering what topics many students would appreciate, take away, build upon, engage with, reflect on and respond to across differences. Next, we will offer a few activities for opening and closing the lesson with positivity.

Opening with Positivity

◆ **Unifying Word:** Present a unifying word to students such as *solidarity, community organizing, allyship*. Students share how they define the term and what it means to them.

◆ **Key Concept:** Extract a key concept that you plan to engage with during your daily lesson. For example, mixed identities may be the focus of your lesson. Ask students to share films, books or other sources that engage that topic.

◆ **Senses and Emotions:** Present a term or concept to students such as *dismantle*. Ask students to evoke their five senses and feelings. When hearing this word, what do they *see, hear, touch, taste, smell, or feel?* Note, students may not be able to relate to every sense.

◆ **Essential questions:** Share your essential questions for today's lesson with students. Ask them to respond to the essential question. Note, their understanding will grow and more knowledge will be added to their understanding as the lesson progresses. *I do not know or I have never thought about it* are acceptable answers.

◆ **Affirmation:** Start the class with a positive affirmation or quote. Everyone says and repeats the affirmation in unison. The affirmation or quote should align with the lesson goals. Twin educators Janelle and Ja'lessa Morris invite a different student in their class each day to present a different quote or affirmation.

◆ **Call and Response:** Start the class with a call and response. Explain the African tradition of call and response. Someone starts the call; the class completes the response. Also, you could have half the class state the call, and the other half states the response. For example, some students will lead with "I come as one." The rest will respond, "But I stand as 10,000."

Closing with Positivity

◆ **Key Takeaway:** Present a key term or concept from the lesson. Students share what they have learned about the concept as a result of the lesson.

◆ **Peers:** After working in small groups or on a class activity, have each student write their name on a post-it or popsicle stick. Students then pick the name of a classmate from a basket. Students share something positive that they gleaned from their classmates.

◆ **Questions:** After the lesson, ask students to share lingering questions that surfaced during the lesson. Educators might ask the following, "If you could speak to the author, filmmaker, songwriter, poet, etc., what question would you pose to that individual and why?"

◆ **Musical Papers** (adapted from Dr. Silvia Bettez, UNC-Greensboro):

◊ Teacher poses a critical question such as, "Write about a time when you witnessed solidarity or allyship."

◊ Students respond anonymously in about a paragraph.

◊ Teacher collects papers.

◊ Teacher passes papers to students randomly.

◊ Students write an affirming comment or question to their peers.

◊ Teacher collects papers and distributes them to different students so that a second response can be written.

◊ After a few shuffles of the papers, the teacher places the anonymous papers on the floor and asks students to come to retrieve their papers.

◊ Students reflect on what has been written.

◆ **Essential Questions:** After the lesson, ask students to return to their original responses to the essential questions. Now that the lesson is complete, ask them to consider how their responses may have shifted from their initial thoughts.

Proficiency Check: For novice learners, present a key term or word and ask them to dramatize or act out the word, expression or emotion. Students can also illustrate what the word represents.

Lesson Plan Theme

Identify the lesson topic, theme or question that is related to race, racism or antiracism. For an antiracist classroom to thrive, educators must overtly incorporate topics related to race, racism and antiracism. The lesson theme or critical question must be race-focused. Antiracist lessons typically fall into one of the following two categories—celebration or education. It is crucial to keep in mind that when teaching for antiracism we must balance topics related to trauma and oppression with those related to joy, culture, celebration and resistance.

Antiracism Takeaway

Identify the antiracist objectives that will be the focus of the lesson. Objectives should describe what students will be able to do upon completion of the lesson. Objectives will relate back to the theme of the lesson, and they should be actionable and deliverable. While antiracist objectives follow the same patterns, they also should include how the lesson has broader implications. Antiracist lessons enrich the world language student and classroom based on at least one of the *Six Dimensions of Antiracism*. A unit of study, in turn, would speak to multiple aspects of the five levels of oppression and change.

Assessment

Ask Yourself!

Consider the following questions for assessing an antiracist lesson.

◆ How does the assessment speak to the antiracist goals of the lesson?
◆ How does the assessment take into consideration the diverse gifts, talents and learning styles of your students?
◆ How does the assessment process help you to reach your goals of combating oppression?
◆ Does the assessment process reinforce oppressions?
◆ Does the assessment consider the variance between heritage speakers and listeners, third culture students, Anglo-speakers, speakers of African American Vernacular English and Chicanx Spanish etc.?

Assessments typically fall into two categories, summative and formative.

Formative Assessment

The goal of formative assessment is to *monitor student learning* to provide ongoing feedback that can be used by instructors to improve their teaching and by students to improve their learning.

More specifically, formative assessments:

◆ help students identify their strengths and weaknesses and target areas that need work;
◆ help faculty recognize where students are struggling and address problems immediately.

Formative assessments are generally *low stakes*, which means that they have low or no point value. Examples of formative assessments include asking students to:

◆ draw a concept map in class to represent their understanding of a topic;
◆ submit one or two sentences identifying the main point of a lecture;
◆ submit a research proposal for early feedback;
◆ submit a draft of a writing assignment for feedback.

Summative Assessment

The goal of summative assessment is to *evaluate student learning* at the end of an instructional unit by comparing it against some standard or benchmark. Summative assessments are often *high stakes*, which means that they have a high point value. Examples of summative assessments include:

◆ a midterm exam
◆ a final project
◆ a paper
◆ a senior recital

Examples of Antiracist Summative Assessments

Within a traditional testing format, we recommend incorporating multiple opportunities for engagement. Krishauna's Spanish Literature students read a passage from *The Souls of Black Folk* by W. E. B. Du Bois (1903) on double consciousness. Du Bois wrote:

> One ever feels his twoness--an American, a Negro; two souls, two thoughts, two unreconciled strivings; two warring ideals in one dark body, whose dogged strength alone keeps it from being torn asunder. The history of the American Negro is the history of this strife--this longing to attain self-conscious manhood, to merge his double self into a better and truer self.

The summative assessment was originally for all students to write a paper explaining the meaning of double consciousness. My student, Aerial Mosley, approached me and asked if she could paint her representation of double consciousness instead of writing a paper. As both a Spanish major and an artist, that was her preferred method of expression and assessment. Wanting to keep all assessments uniform, I initially told her "no", but then thought about her request, and later gave her permission to record her representation on canvas. She still had to write a reflection about her artwork. She produced a solid, sophisticated representation that brought Du Bois' notion of double consciousness to another level, and in turn, her artwork brought her classmates' written work to life. They were able to visualize Du Bois' concept more fully by seeing a visual representation.

Introduction to Spanish Literature: Art Project of Aerial Mosley

Similarly, instead of giving students a traditional text to assess sentence structure, vocabulary use and grammar concepts, you can apply a variety of summative assessments. These include process writing so that students can produce original poetry. For example, when studying physical characteristics, students can read a poem by Spanish poet Gloria Fuertes titled *Yo Soy Así*. A second-year language student produced the following poem. This final product took three drafts, but she produced an original work that represented her lived experiences. Her poem demonstrates mastery of the Spanish language goals which included primarily the use of the verb *ser* (to be), physical descriptions and the literary strategy of repetition.

	Poem by Student Kris Anderson, 3rd semester	Writing Process
Accept me and my imperfections; These are what make me perfect. My hair is not coarse. It is an African crown of glory. My lips are not big, They are only full of passion. My hair is not blond. It is an American Indian kissed by the sun. Accept me and my imperfections; These are what make me perfect. I am a product of my past. Not by selection. Because I, I am weak, but you cannot tell I am shy, but you cannot tell. I am many things, But it does not matter. Accept me and my imperfections; These are what make me perfect.	*Acéptame y mis imperfecciones;* *Estas son las que me hacen perfecto.* *Mi pelo no es áspero.* *Es una corona Africana de gloria.* *Mis labios no son grandes,* *Estos solamente son llenos de pasión,* *Mi pelo no es rubio* *Es un café Amerindio besado por el sol.* *Acéptame y mis imperfecciones;* *Estas son las que me hacen perfecto.* *Yo soy producto de mi pasado,* *No por selección* *Mi sueño es ser más fuerte* *Porque yo,* *Yo soy débil y no lo parece* *Yo soy tímida y no lo parece* *Yo soy muchas cosas,* *Pero no importa,* *Acéptame y mis imperfecciones;* *Estas son las que me hacen perfecto.*	◆ Process Writing: two to three drafts ◆ Title/Repetitive Phrase: What is the essence, personality, voice of the poem. (*Yo soy así*) ◆ Stanza 1: Physical description ◆ Stanza 2: What makes you who you are? What has influenced you? What has shaped you? Give some rationale. ◆ Stanza 3: Describe the intangible traits of your personality. Go deeper, tell us what might not be apparent from simply looking at you. ◆ Instructions: Each stanza has a minimum of three lines. Not necessary to rhyme or have syllabic continuity.

The previous lessons allowed the students to showcase their gifts and talents while also honoring the language and antiracism goals of the class. Educators do not have to sacrifice language outcomes for antiracism. The two can co-exist. German professor, Priscilla Layne, offers the following insights and considerations when incorporating antiracism into daily lessons (personal communication, June 15, 2021).

10 Guidelines for Antiracist Pedagogy

1. **Pay attention to language:** Deconstruct language and compare definitions across languages. For example, what does Diaspora mean in the USA as opposed to Germany? Black out offensive words in historical texts, and only name them by their first letter.
2. **Use texts where minority groups speak for themselves:** Instead of White voices, it is important that students hear from minoritized voices themselves.
3. **Do not [solely] focus on victimization:** Offer stories of empowerment and humor as well.
4. **Do not separate art/literature from the real world:** Art/literature are embedded in real socio-political contexts. Do not treat the text as only interesting because of its political context, pay attention to the aesthetics as well.
5. **Do not marginalize the texts by racialized artists:** Their texts may be a part of the national tradition as well as critiquing it simultaneously. For example, May Ayim's *Autumn in Germany* critiques Germany while also giving voice to Germany's national heritage.
6. **Embrace all forms of media:** Literature, film, music, art and other cultural products.
7. **Decipher slogans:** You can use protest art, signage etc. to draw attention to slogans of the day, and to critique how they speak to current events. Pay attention to when English is used and why.
8. **Current events/local and global:** Give students assignments that allow them to engage actively with the world around them, including social media.

9. **Present diversity in unremarkable and ordinary ways.**
10. **Acknowledge counter histories:** Use readily available materials and current events from newspapers, magazines, music, film, memes and social media. When covering a historical topic in the classroom, it is useful to first consider what the dominant narrative is and what kinds of counternarratives exist.

The following lesson by German Professor, David Limburg, incorporates many of the key tenets shared by Layne.

ANTIRACIST WORLD LANGUAGE LESSON TEMPLATE	
Instructor	David Limburg, Guilford College
Language	German
Language level	Advanced Low
Theme (Include the key, central and/or overarching focus of the lesson or unit.)	Racialized experiences in Germany through the music and writing of Samy Deluxe (Samy Sorge): German Rap Artist, Music Producer, Author
Essential Question(s) (Pose questions that may require more than one lesson, are open-ended, stimulate thought and spark curiosity, concern or inquiry.)	How does creativity become a response to racism in Germany?
Antiracism Takeaway (Key antiracism perspective, understanding or focus)	Racial minorities in Germany find agency through creative expression.
Lesson Objectives and Goals (Upon completion, students will be able to…)	◆ Analyze the lyrics of Samy Deluxe's song.
World Readiness Standards (Include one or more of the *World Readiness Standard* into the lesson or unit plan.)	◆ **Relating Cultural Products to Perspectives:** Learners use the language to investigate, explain and reflect on the relationship between the products and perspectives of the cultures studied. ◆ **Interpretive Communication:** Learners understand, interpret and analyze what is heard, read, or viewed on a variety of topics.

ANTIRACIST WORLD LANGUAGE LESSON TEMPLATE	
Six Dimensions of Antiracism in World Languages (Include one or more of the *Six Dimensions of Antiracism in World Languages* into the lesson or unit plan.)	◆ **Curricular:** Present diverse perspectives, representations and counter stories/counternarratives. ◆ **Curricular:** Incorporate antiracist resources into the world language classroom. ◆ **Curricular:** Incorporate marginalized voices such as Black, Indigenous, Asian, Latinx, people of color, women, LGBTQIA, people with disabilities etc. ◆ **Systemic:** Address how race, ethnicity, racism, antiracism, colorism and other forms of oppression operate on systemic, structural and historical levels.
Activities (Include activities, tasks and engagements that serve to reach the lesson goals, objectives and/or respond to the essential question(s).)	◆ Read excerpt from Samy Deluxe's book *Dis wo ich herkomm* (This is Where I Come From, 2009) at home and come to class prepared to discuss. ◆ Listen to Samy Deluxe's title song track *Dis wo ich herkomm* (same title as book) in class, first with the lyrics sheet and audio alone, then with his music video, without the lyrics sheet. https://vimeo.com/18427427 ◆ Discuss the themes in Deluxe's song.

Assessments (Include summative or formative assessment delineated by communicative, interpretive and/or presentational modes.)	◆ Respond to the following questions.
	  ◆ What does Samy Deluxe criticize about German culture?
	  ◆ What positive aspects does he see in the "New Germany"?
	  ◆ Which lines are most interesting to you and why?
	  ◆ Which lines relate to German history?

ANTIRACIST WORLD LANGUAGE LESSON TEMPLATE	
Homework/Additional Resources	◆ Handout: Review questions from the section on "Heimat" (Home) from Max Frisch's *Fragebogen* (Questionnaire, 1992, Switzerland); Respond to these questions that dive into the topic of feelings and cultural assumptions associated with "home" and "homeland." ◆ Be prepared to discuss the questions in Frisch's chapter. ◆ Transition into a discussion of Samy Deluxe's story as he describes it: born in1977 in Hamburg to a German mother and a Sudanese father, who left the family and returned to Sudan when Deluxe was 2.

ANTIRACIST WORLD LANGUAGE LESSON TEMPLATE	
Instructor	Krishauna Hines-Gaither
Language	French
Language level	Novice Mid
Theme (Include the key, central and/or overarching focus of the lesson or unit.)	Natural hair as resistance to dominant standards and oppressive systems.
Essential Question(s) (Pose questions that may require more than one lesson, are open-ended, stimulate thought and spark curiosity, concern or inquiry.)	◆ How can hair culture serve as a source of pride and resistance?
Antiracism Takeaway (Key antiracism perspective, understanding or focus)	◆ Culturally responsive vocabulary and lessons honor our students' diversity and uniqueness
Lesson Objectives and Goals (Upon completion, students will be able to…)	◆ Examine Black women's experiences and perspectives related to hair. ◆ Understand how hair can be a metaphor for pride and resistance. ◆ Analyze how enslaved Africans used their hair for resistance.

ANTIRACIST WORLD LANGUAGE LESSON TEMPLATE	
World Readiness Standards (Include one or more of the *World Readiness Standards* into the lesson or unit plan.)	◆ **Relating Cultural Products to Perspectives:** Learners use the language to investigate, explain and reflect on the relationship between the products and perspectives of the cultures studied. ◆ **Interpretive Communication:** Learners understand, interpret and analyze what is heard, read, or viewed on a variety of topics. ◆ **Connections:** Learners access and evaluate information and diverse perspectives that are available through the language and its cultures.
Six Dimensions of Antiracism in World Languages (Include one or more of the *Six Dimensions of Antiracism in World Languages* into the lesson or unit plan.)	◆ **Curricular:** Present diverse perspectives, representations and counter stories/counternarratives. ◆ **Curricular:** Incorporate antiracist resources into the world language classroom. ◆ **Curricular:** Incorporate marginalized voices such as Black, Indigenous, Asian, Latinx, people of color, women, LGBTQIA, people with disabilities, etc. ◆ **Systemic:** Address how race, ethnicity, racism, antiracism, colorism and other forms of oppression operate on systemic, structural and historical levels.
Activities (Include activities, tasks and engagements that serve to reach the lesson goals, objectives and/or respond to the essential question(s).)	◆ Watch Nancy Falaise's Workshop video (shorturl.at/bgsAO) on natural hair care in Canada. She will present tips and tools for natural hair in both French and English. ◆ Pay careful attention to the lessons that go beyond hair. What does Falaise share about the following? ◆ *Mots positifs* (Positive ways of describing natural hair) ◆ *Accord* (Consent or in/appropriate touching) ◆ *Estime de soi* (Self-esteem) ◆ *Amour propre* (Self-acceptance) ◆ *Prendre soin de soi* (Self-care)

ANTIRACIST WORLD LANGUAGE LESSON TEMPLATE	
	◆ Create a vocabulary list of words associated with natural hair. ◆ What other French words related to natural hair would you add to the list below that were used in the film? For example, *cheveux frisés, cheveux crépus, tresse*, etc. ◆ Why are these words not included in French textbooks? ◆ Ask students what they think is meant by "protective styling." Many Black students will understand this to mean protecting the hair from breakage by concealing the ends of the hair, typically in an updo. ◆ Read this article and watch this video (shorturl.at/nvGJ7) on how enslaved Africans braided/concealed dry food into their hair for survival when being trafficked from Africa to the Americas/Europe or from plantation to plantation.
Assessments (Include summative or formative assessment delineated by communicative, interpretive and/or presentational modes.)	◆ Students will respond in French or English to the questions posted in the previous section and for homework.

Homework/Additional Resources	◆ Think about different marginalized groups related to LGBTQIA, races/ethnicities, people with disabilities, religions, etc. How have they resisted dominant standards and systems of oppression? Think historically and contemporarily.
	◆ Read excerpt from poem by French poet, Charles Baudelaire, *La Chevelure* (1861).
	    ◆ What are the main points?
	    ◆ What stands out to you?
	    ◆ What ethnicities are referenced?
	    ◆ What similes and metaphors appear in the poem?

ANTIRACIST WORLD LANGUAGE LESSON TEMPLATE	
	Ô toison, moutonnant jusque sur l'encolure! *Ô boucles! Ô parfum chargé de nonchaloir!* *Extase! Pour peupler ce soir l'alcôve obscure* *Des souvenirs dormant dans cette chevelure,* *Je la veux agiter dans l'air comme un mouchoir!*
	O fleecy hair, falling in curls to the shoulders! O black locks! O perfume laden with nonchalance! Ecstasy! To people the dark alcove tonight With memories sleeping in that thick head of hair. I would like to shake it in the air like a scarf!

References

Baudelaire, C. (1861). *La chevelure.* Fleurs du mal. https://fleurs-dumal.org/poem/203

Boyd, L. (2021, April 16). *Flexible lesson planning for world language classes.* Edutopia. www.edutopia.org/article/flexible-lesson-planning-world-language-classes

Du Bois, W.E.B. (1903). *The souls of black folk.* A.C. McClurg & Co.

Shrum, J.L., & Glisan, E.W. (2005). *Teacher's handbook: Contextualized language instruction* (3rd ed.). Thomson Heinle.

6

Addressing Conflicts in the Antiracist Classroom

An essential element to dealing with any conflict in the classroom is a level-headed, calm, approach, and I find this particularly true when the conflict centers around race and racism. These topics are hot-button issues in today's university, and students and instructors alike understand how serious an accusation of racism can be. I feel it is thus important for all involved to take a breath, take a step back, and use the critical thinking skills they have all hopefully been developing up to that point to discuss the incident calmly and openly, with mutual respect.

(John Moran, personal communication,
October 14, 2021)

Courageous Conversations

Throughout this book we have centered the topic of race. Author of the book *Courageous Conversations*, Singleton and Linton (2005) defined courageous conversations as those that:

DOI: 10.4324/9781003218265-7

- ◆ *engage* those who won't talk.
- ◆ *sustain* the conversation when it gets uncomfortable or diverted.
- ◆ *deepen* the conversation to the point where authentic understanding and meaningful actions occur.

(p. 16)

The language classroom offers a space to engage courageous conversations about race. If acknowledged, the foundation of the discipline is racialized. Race, ethnicity, culture and language serve as the spoken or unspoken backdrop of the language classroom. Many language educators teach their subjects from a **race-neutral** paradigm either due to a lack of preparation or fear of getting it wrong. Singleton and Linton report that courageous conversations are directly connected to the achievement gap. Since students of color, and African American students in particular, rank lower on standardized tests, neutrality on race prohibits educators from combating these gaps.

For example, in Chapter 1 we outlined the low numbers of students of color who receive degrees in world languages, hence leading to persistently low numbers of BIPOC in the world language profession. Singleton and Linton counter that if we do not teach about race explicitly, we are unable to address the impact of race and its consequences. Simply put, you cannot resolve a race-based problem with a race-neutral approach. I would also add that the omission of race from the language classroom also cripples educators from celebrating the richness that diversity adds to the classroom.

Courageous Conversations as Opportunity

What if race were the topic that we ran head first into instead of absconding from it? What if we acknowledged that we will likely stumble along the way? Consider a child on the playground who is learning a new game. Most adults would encourage the child to try something new. When the child falls down, we are the first to provide comfort, but the ultimate goal is to get back up and jump right back into the game. This analogy is comparable to the language classroom.

When discussing race, educators may be trying a new skill that requires exercising social, mental and emotional muscles that have not been called upon previously. This is not the time to leave the playground—we encourage language educators to dust off their knees and keep moving along their journeys to antiracism. Mark Chesler of the University of Michigan wrote, "Many faculty are no more **prepared** for the increasing diversity of the academy than are students" (Chesler, 2019, p. 7). Chesler went on to state, "But the opportunity and ability to engage in communication across differences, even controversial or heated ones, is essential in a classroom" (Chesler, 2019, p. 2). Not only are critical conversations advantageous for educators, but also for students.

Beverly Tatum (2019) wrote:

> Colleges and universities are among the few places where people of different racial, cultural, and socioeconomic backgrounds can engage with each other in more than just a superficial way. For many students, regardless of racial background, the college environment is likely the most diverse learning environment they have experienced in their lives.
>
> (p. 80)

We imagine that some K-12 classrooms provide highly diverse environments for students.

In Chapter 1, we discussed the importance of ground rules and offered Sensoy and DiAngelo's 2017 list of conversation starters. In Chapter 5, we discussed opening and closing antiracist lessons on a note of positivity. Now we will offer a few more strategies for engaging in critical conversations.

Activity

The courageous conversation compass helps us to understand the foundation of our conversations. Are you engaging on an intellectual, social, emotional or moral level? This assessment will enable you to gage how you enter a discussion, with what perspective, and for what purpose. When engaging in courageous conversations, assess where your needle is pointing.

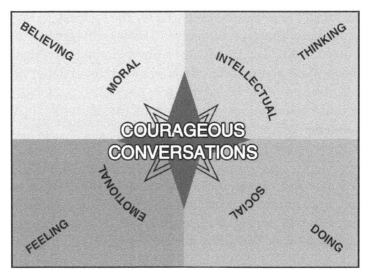

Singleton and Linton, 2005, p. 20

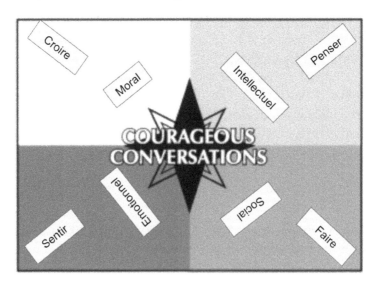

Select a topic and have your students work around the courageous conversation compass.

Topic: Race

1. What do you **believe** the differences or similarities are regarding different races?
2. Why do you **think** that racism exists?
3. How does discussing race make you **feel**?
4. What do you **do** to increase your awareness of race?

Low Risk to High Risk

Present a **low risk topic** to your students, and then as the class or course progresses, introduce higher risk topics. A low-risk topic is one where the stakes are low, there is often a limited emotional response and the level of controversy is minimal. A **high-risk topic** is one where the stakes are higher, there is a stronger emotional response and controversy could ensue. Both low risk and higher risk content are important in the language classroom. This spectrum keeps the language educator from only presenting information on race superficially or at the surface level. Moving up the pendulum to higher risk content brings in deeper reflections and more meaningful engagement. This approach also allows the educator to gage her students' responses and interactions. These observations at lower risk levels can help to inform approaches with higher risk topics.

Critical Moments Defined

After you have had a courageous conversation, it is possible that a critical moment might occur. Glynn et al (2018) stated that **critical moments** have a number of related names, including hot moments (Warren, n.d.) and kairos moments (Bartunek & Carboni, 2006). As Warren (n.d.) states, "Hot moments occur when people's feelings—often conflicting—rise to a point that threatens teaching and learning." Other terms that surfaced in the literature were "difficult moments" (Eberly Center, n.d.) and triggers. Educators should accept that critical moments are a natural part of antiracist pedagogy. As educators and students build trust and community and gain more practice in having courageous conversations, they will better engage and respond to critical moments.

Source of Hot Moments

When we are discussing issues related to racism and/or anti-racism it is very common to have critical moments in the class-room. What do we mean by critical or hot moments? What are they and where do they come from? Hot moments can be evoked from any source (faculty, staff, students, adminis-trators, social media, community, media, etc.), on any topic and from any identity group. Everyone is capable of evoking a critical moment. Hot moments are instances where conver-sation gets heated in the classroom, or at other times the hot moment may evoke silence—as the old expression goes, "the air was sucked out of the room." Hot moments can be initiated by either a comment or an action that causes offense or hurt (Eberly Center, n.d., para 3). The following are common sources of hot moments:

◆ comments shared or actions committed before the entire class;
◆ small group comments or actions;
◆ issues that occur within the school community that leak into the classroom (may occur in the hallway, in another class, on the playground, during extracurricular activi-ties, on the school bus, at the bus stop, in the neighbor-hood, etc.);
◆ classroom norms, codes, culture;
◆ sensitive topics or current events prevalent in the local, national, or international news media;

- ◆ social media posts, memes, shares, likes and/or exchanges that leak into the classroom;
- ◆ course content that a student may deem problematic (reading, film);
- ◆ calling someone out;
- ◆ microaggressions such as micro assaults, microinsults and/or microinvalidations;
- ◆ passive aggressive behaviors.

Are Hot Moments Always Negative?

Although critical moments typically have a negative connotation due to the discomfort that they evoke, they can also be induced by laudable intentions. For example, a student who openly questions why the instructor does not have any readings on the syllabus from Indigenous authors or LGBTQIA communities may have noble intentions of inclusion; however, the inquiry may be met with defensiveness from the instructor and cause tension. Instructors can also be on the receiving end of hot moments.

Hot Moments Resulting from Microaggressions

Contributors to this book reported hot moments in a variety of contexts. For example, one educator stated, "As a teacher, I have encountered students laughing at my accent when speaking English. I ignored it and focused on my instruction." Sue and colleagues (2010) found that a common precipitator of difficult dialogues or hot moments is **microaggressions**. Any marginalized group may experience microaggressions based on their race, religion, gender, sexual orientation, size, disability, etc. There are three forms of microaggressions: microinsult, micro assault and microinvalidation. Examples of each follow.

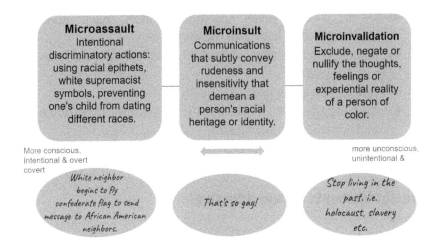

Microassault
Intentional discriminatory actions: using racial epithets, white supremacist symbols, preventing one's child from dating different races.

Microinsult
Communications that subtly convey rudeness and insensitivity that demean a person's racial heritage or identity.

Microinvalidation
Exclude, negate or nullify the thoughts, feelings or experiential reality of a person of color.

More conscious, Intentional & overt covert

more unconscious, unintentional &

White neighbor begins to fly confederate flag to send message to African American neighbors.

That's so gay!

Stop living in the past. i.e. holocaust, slavery etc.

Educators who are not aware of these behaviors can inadvertently perpetuate the problematic actions, or worse, leave them unaddressed. The following are other examples of hot moments that contributors to this text reported.

Microinsult: "I showed a picture of a Latinx woman riding a donkey, and asked students to discuss the role of animals in different societies. A White male student responded, 'Which one is the donkey.'"

Mistrust: "I incorporated Afro-Latinx content into my Spanish class. I only had two African American students in the class. As a White professor, they were actually offended, questioned my motives, and said that I was trying too hard."

Microassault: "My White professor said the N-word in class with no abbreviation (said complete word instead of abbreviating it). She said the whole word. She said that she could say it because she was reading it from a historical text." I walked out and immediately dropped the class."

Microinsult/Microinvalidation: "When I was teaching about LGBT allyship, a Black male student said, 'If a lesbian found a good man, she wouldn't be gay for long.'"

Call out: "It is exhausting when White people sit in these spaces where people of color are always the ones speaking about race or injustice. White people need to contribute to these spaces, too. Why aren't you saying anything?"

Microinsult/Microinvalidation: "My middle school Spanish teacher was White from the United States, although she studied in Spain. The first day of class, the teacher asked me if I had any knowledge of Spanish. I said yes, and spoke a little to her. She said, "Who taught you this slang?" I said, "My *buela* says this to me all the time." She responded, "Well that is not correct, your ABUELA (correcting me) does not know what she is talking about." I cried because that's my grandmother, you can't say that she doesn't know her language."

Passive aggression/Microinvalidation:
"When I did not want to hear what students of color had to say about their experiences with racism, I would get on my phone, look out the window, or play with my papers. They told the teacher, but she didn't believe them." White female student

Read the quotes and discuss the following questions:

1. What might be the motivation behind the scenarios?
2. Could the hot moment have been avoided? If so, how?
3. How would you have reacted or addressed the situation?
4. What are some lessons that instructors can learn from these hot moments?
5. Could you think of a hot moment that happened in your own classroom or when you were a student?
6. What are the preparatory steps that educators can take before a critical moment occurs?

Target Language First Approach

At novice levels, the instructor might teach students possible responses to hot moments. These responses may include cognates that are easily recognizable at the novice levels or images for logographic languages. Students do not have to understand all constructions of the following phrases, but the meaning will be clear by the cognates. For languages that do not have recognizable cognates to the first language, draft short concise statements, post them in your classroom and practice them with your students until they become automatized.

Reflection Statements

- *pausa* (Pause.)
- *tranquila* (Take a moment.)

- ◆ *respira* (Breathe.)
- ◆ *considera el impacto* (Consider the impact.)

Stronger Statements

- ◆ *Favor de/Hay que respetar.* (Show respect.)
- ◆ *Favor de/Hay que estar presente.* (Be present.)
- ◆ *Favor de/Hay que prestar atención.* (Pay attention.)
- ◆ *Es una falta de respeto.* (That is a lack of respect.)
- ◆ *No lo digas. No digas eso.* (Do not say that.)

For intermediate and advanced levels, you might use the same expressions as above, but add more information on why the hot moment occurred and its impact. Those follow-up conversations can take place in the target language.

Another option at novice levels is an L1 ticket. So that students honor the target language, educators can use a phrase that indicates that one needs to speak in English. For example, *"En inglés por favor* (in English please)." Although what follows is in English, the students are providing a lead-in in the target language.

Safety over Target Language

Although we affirm the importance of the target language, we do not do so at all costs. If the classroom environment is not conducive to learning because the facilitator has failed to address hot moments, this environment impedes target language instruction. Our position is that unaddressed hot moments do not foster a classroom where language learning is optimized. For this reason, it is more advantageous to come out of the target language, if necessary, to reset the classroom. In doing so, students' psychosocial needs are met and the awkward tension is addressed. With this approach, the repair work can begin.

Prepare for Conflict in Times of Peace

Consider Your Own Biases

Everyone has biases. In order to work towards an antiracist classroom, it is important for educators to self reflect and examine their own biases. Engage in thoughtful exercises where both educators and students can consider their biases. Just as a skilled facilitator can put participants on a path to self-awareness through training, so can the world language educator. For example, educators and students can join the over 5,000 people globally who have taken Harvard's Implicit Associations Test (https://tinyurl.com/bdz54xhf). This test can be a good way to start the reflective process related to bias. Other helpful resources follow.

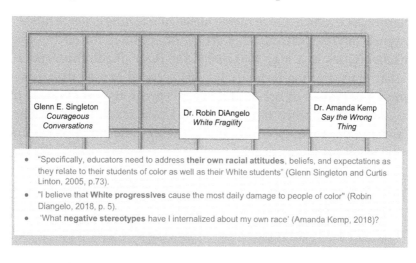

Glenn E. Singleton
Courageous Conversations

Dr. Robin DiAngelo
White Fragility

Dr. Amanda Kemp
Say the Wrong Thing

- "Specifically, educators need to address **their own racial attitudes**, beliefs, and expectations as they relate to their students of color as well as their White students" (Glenn Singleton and Curtis Linton, 2005, p.73).
- "I believe that **White progressives** cause the most daily damage to people of color" (Robin Diangelo, 2018, p. 5).
- 'What **negative stereotypes** have I internalized about my own race' (Amanda Kemp, 2018)?

Survey the Class in Advance

Ask students at the onset of class, if something offensive occurs, how would they like for it to be addressed? This can be done via written responses that are submitted to the instructor, or as a whole class discussion. When Silvia Bettez, Department of Education faculty at the University of North Carolina-Greensboro did this exercise with her students, one student responded that if she said something problematic, she did not want anyone to address it. When Silvia asked if the class could agree to that, no one could. The class discussed it and the student understood the various perspectives of her classmates. Although all preferences may not be honored, it is still helpful to the instructor to have a pulse of the students' expectations and preferences.

Discuss Community

Discuss the type of community that you wish to create. One good leading statement could be, "We would like to have a classroom in which…" Have each student respond to this question.

Pre-reading

Before a critical moment occurs, offer your students different tools to help them to address concerns. One article that may be helpful is Loretta Ross' *Speaking up without tearing down* (https://tinyurl.com/yc55etmy). This article offers tools for addressing insensitivities in a way that opens the door of communication, rather than shutting it down. It is also crucial to note that sometimes a comment or action may be so egregious that it needs to be shut down rather than engaged. Upon reading this article, Krishauna's students wrote the following reflections. What are your reactions to this article?

"The term 'calling-in' was a new term for me, so when I began reading I didn't know what to think. When she began to explain the negative impacts of calling out, such as causing a bigger conflict with nothing left to learn, I started to understand how calling-in works." Lacey-Ann Reynolds

"It is hard, though, when someone says something harmful against a marginalized group in which you belong, and to use the call-in method, because your immediate reaction is to be mad. So I understand that too." Annie Degraffenried

Engage in Cross-Racial Dialogues

Empirical data from the University of Michigan, Skidmore College and others have found that students from high school to college levels who engage in cross-racial dialogues "deepened their ability to think critically about racial issues and listen actively to others' opinions" (Tatum, 2019, p. 85). Although the data is based on well facilitated and organized programs, equally important is attendance in multicultural spaces where your personal identity may not be centered. This exposure builds your capacity to engage in hot moments, should they occur, and meaningful discussions across differences.

Have Co-Constructed Ground Rules

As discussed in Chapter 1, ground rules serve to gird the antiracist classroom. Knepp (2012) suggested engaging students in the co-creation of a classroom code, having them talk openly about the kind of classroom environment that would work best for them, and especially one that might work best in difficult situations or for controversial topics. Since most language educators have not been trained extensively in diversity, equity and inclusion, we recommend that educators be open to the co-construction of knowledge. Students and their communities can fill gaps where educators and course content may be lacking.

Create Content That Centers Critical Moments

One way to build capacity to engage with critical moments is to allow students the opportunity to engage in hot topics. Using pop culture examples can allow students to engage in discussions of critical content without speaking directly to an individual student's experience. What can be learned or gleaned from these experiences that may be helpful in the classroom? At a program at Guilford College, students reviewed insensitive comments made by celebrities based on race, gender, sexuality and more. In the examples, several students felt that it was common for celebrities not to take full responsibility for their actions. Their apologies seemed insincere.

Considerations for Addressing Critical Moments

Pasque, P., Charbeneau, J., Chesler, M., & Carlson, C (2013) indicate that some faculty address conflict in the following ways. Faculty may…

- ◆ stop conflict and incivility immediately upon its occurrence;
- ◆ permit it to surface, but try to control it;
- ◆ try to use it as a means for teaching students how to work across boundaries and differences in more civil ways;
- ◆ even deliberately create learning designs (curricular and pedagogical practices) that proactively surface or generate dissonance, and follow with instruction on how students can learn from such encounters.

Pasque et al. concluded, "Above all, faculty should not ignore, overlook or avoid dealing with incivilities that occur." However, not all critical moments will be addressed in the same manner. Assessing each situation will be critical in determining the best course of action. Some considerations follow:

1. Did it occur in front of the entire class?
2. Did it take place in a small group?
3. Did it occur inside or outside of the classroom?
4. Did it happen within the same identity group or between different identity groups?
5. At what point in the class did the critical moment occur (beginning, middle, end)?
6. Who was the source of the critical moment: student, staff, faculty, administrator?
7. How did it impact the class or individual(s)?
8. What will be the impact on the affected party or parties if the matter is, or is not, addressed?
9. What if the victim who was directly targeted prefers that the matter is not addressed?
10. What are some of the ways you can reach out to ensure that the person who was the target of the incivility can discuss it later if they choose?

None of the above queries should prohibit a faculty member from addressing a hot moment; but considering these questions can allow for a more thoughtful response, and may decrease the potential to cause unintended harm.

Ask Yourself!

Think about how you address critical moments.

- ◆ Can you think of a critical moment that took place in your class within the last year?
- ◆ How did you handle it?
- ◆ What do you think you did well?
- ◆ What could you have improved upon in your response?

We offer the following strategies for responding to a hot moment.

Effective Dialogue Skills: PAIRS

P: Pan the environment and yourself (Pay Attention Now); What do you notice?

A: Ask about the specifics behind the comment or behavior.

I: Interrupt the dynamics; slow down, pause.

R: Relate to the person or their comment.

S: Share about yourself; self-disclose a story, your feelings, the impact of the comment.

Kathy Obear, Center for Transformation and Change

Strategies for Responding to Hot Moments	Examples
Name what has taken place	"There seems to have been a reaction to what was just said. How did you receive that comment?"
Assign a free write exercise	"So that we can have more time to process what just happened, write a paragraph describing how you are feeling." These can be handed in or not; discussed or not.
Respond with facts	Offer data to combat misinformation.
Give yourself distance	Give yourself some space before addressing the hot moment if it is triggering for you, or if you are too upset to offer a productive response.
Address in small groups	It may be helpful to speak with students in smaller groups if the matter occurred in a small group setting.
Address in large group	If the hot moment happened in front of the entire class, and if you deem it would be harmful to leave the matter unaddressed, it may be a good idea to address the full group.
Role-play	Have students role-play a critical moment. Leave it unresolved. Invite the other students to determine how they might address that critical moment.

References

Banks, B.M., Adams, D.F., Williams, C. & Piña, D. (2020). Preliminary investigation of efforts to improve awareness of racial microaggressions on campus. *Journal of Underrepresented and Minority Progress*, 4(1), 20–43.

Bartunek, J. M., & Carboni, I. (2006). A time for hope: A response to Nancy Adler. *Academy of Management Learning and Education*, 5(4), 500–504.

Chesler, M. (2019). What is incivility in the academic environment? And what can we do about it? With particular attention to race and gender equity concerns. Working Paper No. 8. https://drive.google.com/file/d/1vdcgnV2SUipCK8qbNQ6PXizDoNohoVbP/view

Eberly Center: Teaching Excellence and Educational Innovation. (n.d.) *Handle difficult moments with respect and sensitivity*. Carnegie Mellon University. www.cmu.edu/teaching/designteach/teach/classroomclimate/handledifficultmoments.html

Glenn, S.E., & Linton, C. (2005). *Courageous conversations about race: A field guide for achieving equity in schools*. Corwin Press.

Glynn, C., Wesely, P., Wassell, B. (2018). *Words and actions: Teaching languages through the lens of social justice* (2nd ed.). The American Council on the Teaching of Foreign Languages.

Knepp, K.A.F. (2012). Understanding student and faculty incivility in higher education. *The Journal of Effective Teaching*, 12(1), 32–45.

Pasque, P., Charbeneau, J., Chesler, M., & Carlson, C. (2013). Pedagogical approaches to racial conflict in the classroom. *Journal of Diversity in Higher Education*. 6(1), 1–16.

Sensoy, Ö., & DiAngelo, R. (2017). *Is everyone really equal? An introduction to key concepts in social justice education* (2nd ed.). Teachers College Press.

Sue, D.W. (2010, November 17). Microaggressions: More than just race. *Psychology Today*. www.psychologytoday.com/us/blog/microaggressions-in-everyday-life/201011/microaggressions-more-just-race

Tatum, B.D. (2019). Together and alone? The challenge of talking about racism on campus. *Dædalus, Journal of the American Academy of Arts and Sciences*, 148(4), 79–93

Warren, L. & Derek Bok Center. (n.d.). Managing hot moments in the classroom. www.elon.edu/u/academics/catl/wp-content/uploads/sites/126/2017/04/Managing-Hot-Moments-in-the-Classroom-Harvard_University.pdf

7

Teaching Antiracism across Proficiency Levels

Language and education are mutually inclusive: language is developed through education which, in turn, is accessed via language. It is central to the process of learning; it is the vehicle by which language itself is taught and through which content of subjects are taught. It is the medium through which we learn about social justice; and thereby becomes an important empowering tool with which to question and investigate; to be critically literate; to challenge and protest; to argue and debate; to ask why and why not? This is the language of social justice.

(Stephen Campitelli, ESL/EFL, RMIT University
and the University of Melbourne)

ACTFL recommends that educators teach in the target language 90% or more of classroom time with the exception of immersion program models where the expectation is to teach exclusively in the target language. The goal is to provide immersion in the target language unless the educators have a viable reason to NOT use the target language. While it is possible to offer meaningful target language instruction at the novice levels in antiracism, due

DOI: 10.4324/9781003218265-8

to limited linguistic resources at the novice level, educators will need to be flexible with teaching exclusively in the target language. Per the backward design model, it is important to assess your lesson objectives, the evidence needed to support the lesson goals and classroom activities. In planning, educators should assess their intentions and the impact on student learning.

Ask Yourself!

◆ Can I teach this antiracist lesson almost exclusively in the target language and provide comprehensible input for my students?
◆ Will my students be able to reach the goals of the lesson if instruction is 90% in the target language?
◆ Will students have equitable opportunities to engage in the lesson if taught exclusively in the target language?
◆ What will be gained versus what will be lost if the lesson is reliant upon the target language?
◆ Who is advantaged versus who is disadvantaged by my instructional language choice?
◆ Are the antiracist objectives important enough for me to come out of the target language?

Increasing oral proficiency in the classroom requires **comprehensible input**. Spanish teacher Adriana Ramírez stated:

I teach using Comprehensible Input methodologies. I teach with stories. I make sure I include different characters, pictures and videos in my stories. I make sure I include different experiences. I make sure the White experience is decentered from the beginning. The more language they have acquired, the more in depth we can go.

Since students are not totally immersed, they need a simulation of the immersion experience in order to gain enough second language input to produce target language output. Additionally, students also need comprehensible input in relation to antiracism. If the educator presents a dynamic lesson on antiracism, yet students cannot understand it due to the language barrier, what has really been gained? Conversely, if the instructor can teach the lesson in the target language while ensuring comprehensibility, by all means we support that approach. Shrum and Glisan explained as follows:

> Keeping the languages separate results in more proficiency achievement than mixing them or translating them. Spanish teacher, Ms. Loria, gives simple instructions in Spanish for classroom activities and does not translate them into English. If her students know that she will supply the English after the Spanish instructions, they stop listening to the Spanish. Ms. Loria also said that if she knows she is not going to use English, she puts more thought into making the input comprehensible.
>
> (p. 150)

One can create an antiracist classroom at all levels of proficiency both in the target language and in English. Educators will need to thoughtfully consider that even if some English is needed, with antiracist lessons students are still on task. English instruction still honors the target language and antiracism goals by bringing in elements that are not otherwise fully accessible to the students due to their limited linguistic resources. The lesson approach and preparation will differ based upon the students' proficiency levels.

Reading Proficiency

Shrum and Glisan (2010, p. 150) suggest that educators "edit the task, but not the text," meaning do not alter the authentic resource. Rather, alter what you do with the text if students need more support to be able to engage with it. Spanish teacher Maris Hawkins (2017) offers an alternative perspective. While she sees the value of authentic resources, she shared: "Students can quickly become overwhelmed with the amount of text that they do not understand…Instead of eliminating authentic resources or continuing to frustrate students, there is another solution! EDIT the TEXT" (paras 4 & 5, author's emphasis). We agree that while authentic texts are important at all levels of instruction, educators may need to pair them down to a developmentally appropriate level. Above all, we recommend that educators include literature, art, music, history, sociology, science and the like at all proficiency levels, even novice levels. Here is how:

Present students with one stanza from a poem or an excerpt from a song. Focus their attention on key elements of the song. This song titled *Paris Sera Toujours Paris* was first published in 1939 during a time of conflict between Germany and France, and Zaz covered the song in 2014 (Zaz, 2014). How do these lyrics relate to the coronavirus or other events of today?

Proficiency Check: For novice levels, start with cognates and ask students to discuss what comes to mind when they think of words like *le masque à gaz*.

Pour qu'à ce bruit chacun s'entraîne *On peut la nuit jouer **d'la sirène*** *Nous contraindre à faire le zouave*	To prepare everyone for the sound We play sirens at night Restrain ourselves to playing the fool
*En **pyjama** dans notre **cave*** *On aura beau par **des ukases*** *Nous couper l'veau et même **le jazz***	In pajamas in our basements We've had enough of decrees That would ban our veal and even jazz
*Nous **imposer le masque à gaz*** *Des mots croisés à quatre cases*	Tell us to wear gas masks Limit our crosswords to four squares
*Nous **obliger** dans nos **demeures*** *A nous **coucher** tous à **onze heures***	Command us in our homes To be in bed by eleven

Novice Proficiency Levels		
Automatization	Teachers should establish common terms and vocabulary that will be regularly accessed when teaching on antiracism. For example, from day one, students learn greetings and salutations and imperatives such as "raise your hand", open your book", "no English please", etc. Incorporate useful phrases from day one that honor antiracism. The more they are used, the more *automatized* they will become.	◆ These statements can be your community guidelines. ◆ I want to hear different perspectives. ◆ Speak one at a time.

Novice Proficiency Levels		
Conversation starters	Offer students conversation starters as outlined in Chapter 1. These starters will offer students a chance to get their juices flowing in the target language.	Teach conversation starters such as ◆ In my opinion… ◆ Being Asian… ◆ In my community…
Provide an egress	Allow students to speak in English, while still honoring the target language.	Students earn tickets by speaking in the target language, even if they are inaccurate. They can use their tickets when they need to speak in English. Teach students to ask permission in the target language to speak in English. They might use phrases such as… ◆ In English please? ◆ May I speak in English? ◆ May I? (Adapted from Spanish teacher, Susan Keener.)
Sacred time	Consider a certain portion of the day when you will incorporate an English-only lesson.	This portion may be the first 15 minutes, last 20 minutes of class. It may also be a particular day of the week. It may also be the entire class period.

In world language in elementary school, classrooms consider cultural lessons that students can engage in. Here are some ideas. Use cultural symbols to engage intersectional identities. Educators might use the Pride flag of the LGBTQIA community to teach or to introduce colors. You can use the following symbols to teach colors.

Cultural Symbols and Descriptions	Teaching points
	Use flags to teach colors and to represent different identities of the target language. Also, note how people often use flags to honor their culture, ethnicity, nationality and heritage, or to draw attention to a social concern.
	Use flags to teach about social concerns. Discuss how different causes are important to different people. Advocates will often use a flag as a symbol of their concern or cause.

Teaching a language is very rewarding, especially when we see how students move from one proficiency level to another and how they begin to express themselves in the target language. However, ensuring that students are proficient in the cultures of the language we teach is just as valuable and rewarding. Attention to cultural proficiency will help to create an antiracist world language classroom. Thus, it is critical that instructors reimagine proficiency not just in terms of students being able to express themselves grammatically, but also culturally.

When using the term *culture* we are referring to an umbrella term, which includes social behaviors and norms that are present in different societies. This may include, but is not limited to, arts, customs, social institutions such as religion, social identities such as race, ethnicity, sexuality, gender, ability, class and other identity markers. When we talk about culture we can also allude to a specific time, place or social context whereby people navigate and interact with one another. However, most often when the language profession refers to proficiency, there is an increased focus on linguistic competence, and to a lesser degree, cultural competence.

Missing Alignment between Language and Antiracism Proficiencies

According to the ACTFL Performance Descriptors for Language Learners:

> Proficiency is the ability to use language in real world situations in a spontaneous interaction and non-rehearsed context and in a manner acceptable and appropriate to native speakers of the language. Proficiency demonstrates what a language user is able to do regardless of where, when or how the language was acquired.
>
> (ACTFL, 2015, p. 4)

The language proficiency goals are clearly outlined in the ACTFL *Proficiency Guidelines* (2012) and the aforementioned Performance Descriptors. The WRS for Learning Languages provide a reference point for culture in that learners should "interact with cultural competence and understanding." Language educators can access a number of resources to ground language proficiency and cultural proficiency; however, the gap that currently exists is the absence of direct communication between language proficiency and antiracism and/or social justice proficiency.

Jean Rueckert (2021, p. 28), Director of World Languages at the American Community School of Abu Dhabi wrote, "I recognize that the [language] community must first speak the same language about developing proficiency." The two paradigms of language and antiracism lack intertextuality in that one does not speak to the other. While resources abound to address language proficiency, we are devoid of a comparable model to address antiracism. Many language educators adopted the *Social Justice*

Standards: The Teaching Tolerance Anti-Bias Framework (Teaching Tolerance, 2016). These standards certainly move us closer in harmony with antiracism, but they too miss the mark. The four anchor standards and domains (identity, diversity, justice and action) do not mention race, racism, ethnicity or antiracism.

Professor and Director of the Second Language Teaching and Research Center at the University of Utah, Fernando Rubio, calls for greater alignment of proficiency aims. Rubio (2021) emphasized "the need to align assessment with teaching and learning… and the need to realign and adjust proficiency goals based on evidence received from assessments" (p. 16). In the absence of a model that connects language proficiency to antiracism, we yield to Rubio's assertion that educators must be flexible and adapt to make adjustments to reach antiracist proficiency outcomes.

What Is the Goal of the Language Classroom?

Manuela Wagner, Associate Professor of Foreign Language Education and Director of the German Language and Culture Program at the University of Connecticut, facilitated a webinar for the Center for Educational Resources in Culture, Language and Literacy. During her webinar she took a deeper look at the concept of proficiency. Wagner (2021) asked, "Should language education go beyond the goal of teaching language proficiency? If so, what are some objectives of language education beyond language proficiency?" The virtual audience of language educators responded resoundingly that language proficiency should *not* be the only goal of the language classroom. Other objectives that the audience mentioned follow:

Ask Yourself!

◆ What are the goals of the language classroom beyond language proficiency? What would you add to this list?
◆ Ask your students to respond to these questions on day one:
   ◆ What is your goal for taking this class?
   ◆ What do you hope to receive from this class?
   ◆ How can this class help you to reach your goals?

Affirm Both Classroom and Personal Goals

After you and your students respond to the *Ask Yourself* questions, share your goals as an educator and have students share their goals. You can then discuss some tips and tools for how students can reach classroom aims, and also how they might reach their individual goals. This approach will indicate that students also have active roles in the language learning process as well as the educator. For example, a student might respond, "I want to be able to speak with kids who speak a certain language in my neighborhood." Based on their responses, students can draft three ways that they can make steps toward reaching that goal. Teachers can have check-ins with students on their progress.

Although students may not be fluent enough during the course of your class to have complex conversations, they can make progress towards their goals.

Proficiency Check: Novice speakers can learn essential greetings in order to greet heritage and native speakers in their neighborhoods in the target language.

◆ Intermediate speakers can converse with heritage and native speakers in their neighborhoods in different tenses. If they have been speaking more in the present tense, they might challenge themselves to speak in the past tense.
◆ Based on the country of origin or influence, advanced speakers might learn from their heritage and native speaker peers different ways of saying what they have learned in class or different vocabulary.

Another common reason that students take language courses is because the course is a graduation or college admittance requirement. Receiving course credit can be a strong motivator as well. Students need to be set up for success in order to reach these goals. Educators might offer tips for how to be successful in the language classroom. Oftentimes students have not received helpful instruction on how language learning takes shape, as well as the benefits. Languages are often presented to students as either inaccessible (difficult, challenging, for a select few) or as the fulfillment of a curriculum requirement (just take two units and you're done). Educators can balance this misalignment by bringing a healthy discussion of proficiency into the world language classroom. Let us demystify proficiency by sharing language learning strategies and benefits with our students from a value-added and not a deficit-based perspective. Some examples follow.

Ask Yourself!

Depending on your language context, what are additional tips that you might add to this list?

1. Acquiring a language is not dependent on unique gifts or talents. Like any other subject, with good instruction and practice, you can learn a language!
2. You already possess strengths that will help you to learn a language.
3. There is always something more to learn when it comes to language study.
4. Language study enables us to understand different cultures and to build relationships with global communities.
5. Consider the classroom as a community. How can each student and teacher create an environment where you thrive?
6. Engage resources and study tools early so that they can assist with the language learning process.
7. Language learning is a cumulative process whereby one skill or lesson will build upon the next one.
8. If you find a topic challenging, get help immediately, get help early.
9. Language learning includes reading, writing, speaking and listening.
10. Proficiency in a language will take commitment outside of class. Expect to spend __ amount of time studying your language each week.

On the Web

◆ Visit Lead with Languages for their Top ten reasons to learn languages. www.leadwithlanguages.org/why-learn-languages/top-ten-reasons-to-learn-languages/

How Does Antiracism Affirm Language Proficiency Goals?

Research (Ladson-Billings, 1995; Delpit, 2006) shows that when learning is **connected** to students' personal lives and home communities, they are more engaged. Antiracism is an avenue to connect to students and their communities, and thereby increase student motivation and engagement. Since language learning is not the only goal of the language classroom, an antiracist framework can enable educators to reach **goals** of community-building, identity development, critical thinking, social justice, intersectionality, global awareness, cross-cultural understanding and antiracism. Antiracist instruction enhances the teaching of **culture**. **Contextualized** antiracist lessons that follow the backward design model and that include the *Six Dimensions of Antiracism in World Languages* provide a solid grounding for cultural inquiry. When the language lessons are thought-provoking, not surface level or superficial, they can be conduits to **deeper reflections**.

For example, lower-level engagement may be a lesson related to representation. While it is vitally important to have different identities represented in the language classroom, it is also essential to consider how history, structures, society, curriculum, etc., align or impact those who are represented. Like any lesson plan, the level of antiracist engagement will depend on the developmental level of the students. When educators thoughtfully incorporate antiracism, they will offer a more **complex analysis** that embeds less superficial treatment, hence building greater levels of critical engagement. L. J. Randolph (2021) warned that it is dangerous to have an "attempt at representation with no critical lens."

Towards Antiracist Proficiency

What does it mean for students to be proficient in antiracism? We return to the four stages of intergroup dialogue as outlined in detail with examples in Chapter 2: 1) ensure that students are building trust and community from the beginning; 2) include strong attention to identity with a centering of race and its inter-sections; 3) discuss critical social topics that offer deeper cul-tural and antiracist awareness; 4) finally, these stages should seek to build alliances, bridges and a commitment to continue engaging in antiracism. Use the *Six Dimensions of Antiracism* to ground your lessons and approaches to antiracism. These stages and dimensions will provide ample framework to assess profi-ciency in antiracism. Some considerations follow for antiracist proficiency.

◆ **Become proficient in multiple dimensions of anti-racism:** Include opportunities to assess antiracist profi-ciency at various levels including personal, interpersonal, cultural, curricular, institutional and systemic.

◆ **Understand the target cultures that are represented:** Include members of the target culture who are in the majority as well as minoritized cultures such as Black, Indigenous, Women, LGBTQIA, people with disabilities (differently abled), gender diversity, etc.

◆ **Address current events and hot topics:** Be aware of cur-rent events as they relate to race, racism, colorism and antiracism. Include events in lessons, units of study and discussions.

◆ **Provide linguistic resources:** Use a scaffolded approach so that students at various proficiency levels have the necessary linguistic tools to engage in meaningful discussions.

◆ **Be flexible:** Honor the experiences of minoritized indi-viduals by allowing students to engage in critical conver-sations in the target language or in English.

ANTIRACIST WORLD LANGUAGE LESSON TEMPLATE	
Instructor	Cécile Accilien
Language	French
Language level	Intermediate Mid

ANTIRACIST WORLD LANGUAGE LESSON TEMPLATE	
Theme (Include the key, central and/or overarching focus of the lesson or unit.)	Racism in France and its Enduring Legacies
Essential Question(s) (Pose questions that may require more than one lesson, are open-ended, stimulate thought and spark curiosity, concern or inquiry.)	1. What are the perceptions of French people regarding African intellectualism? 2. What is the relationship between Francophone African countries and France? 3. What is the relationship between Anglophone African nations and France? 4. What role do race and nationality have on the travel experiences of tourists in France?
Antiracism Takeaway (Key antiracism perspective, understanding or focus)	◆ The history of France as a colonial power on the African continent still has enduring legacies of racism and classism. ◆ The notion of the French as a republic where everyone is supposedly equal prevents people from having sustainable and honest conversations about race in France.
Lesson Objectives and Goals (Upon completion, students will be able to…)	◆ Have conversation in French about the relationship and perception of race and class between France and African countries. ◆ Have conversation with peers about the complexity of racism in their communities and compare and contrast it with the ways it is manifested in France or a French-speaking region.
World Readiness Standards (Include one or more of the *World Readiness Standards* into the lesson or unit plan.)	**Interpersonal Communication:** Learners interact and negotiate meaning in spoken, signed, or written conversations to share information, reactions, feelings and opinions. **Interpretive Communication:** Learners understand, interpret and analyze what is heard, read, or viewed on a variety of topics.

ANTIRACIST WORLD LANGUAGE LESSON TEMPLATE	
	Presentational Communication: Learners present information, concepts and ideas to inform, explain, persuade and narrate on a variety of topics using appropriate media and adapting to various audiences of listeners, readers or viewers
	Cultures:
	Relating Cultural Practices to Perspectives: Learners use the language to investigate, explain and reflect on the relationship between the practices and perspectives of the cultures studied.
	Relating Cultural Products to Perspectives: Learners use the language to investigate, explain and reflect on the relationship between the products and perspectives of the cultures studied.
	Cultural Comparisons:
	Learners use the language to investigate, explain and reflect on the concept of culture through comparisons of the cultures studied and their own.
Language Goal	What are some of the ways we can use cognates to help students use antiracist vocabulary to write about inequities in the French speaking world?
Six Dimensions of Antiracism in World Languages (Include one or more of the *Six Dimensions of Antiracism in World Languages* into the lesson or unit plan.)	◆ **Personal/Individual:** Address how race, ethnicity, racism, antiracism and other forms of oppression operate on a personal level. ◆ **Interpersonal:** Address how race, ethnicity, racism, antiracism and other forms of oppression operate on an interpersonal level. ◆ **Cultural/Societal:** Address how race, ethnicity, racism, antiracism and other forms of oppression operate on cultural and societal levels

ANTIRACIST WORLD LANGUAGE LESSON TEMPLATE	
Activities (Include activities, tasks and engagements that serve to reach the lesson goals, objectives and/or respond to the essential question(s).)	◆ **Pre-Viewing:** Instructor will present a list of cognates that relate to the videos, many of the vocabulary words will be used in the videos. The instructor will first present the list in context in alignment with Shrum and Glisan's contextualized language teaching. ◆ **Example:** *Pour comprendre la discrimination raciale en France il faut prendre en compte certains faits historiques. Par exemple, la France a eu des colonies en Amérique, en Asie et en Afrique. Elle a eu une approche colonisatrice en s'appuyant sur une mission "civilisatrice" et éducatrice. La France a toujours des départements et territoires d'outre-mer (DOM-TOM): La Guyane, La Guadeloupe, la Réunion, la Martinique, la Polynésie française, la Mayotte, Wallis et Futuna, Saint-Pierre et Miquelon et la Nouvelle-Calédonie.* ◆ [In order to understand racial discrimination in France we must take into account certain historical facts. For example, France had colonies in the Americas, Asia and Africa. It had a colonizing approach while leaning on the idea of "civilizing" and educating the Native inhabitants. France still has overseas departments and territories (DOM-TOM): Guyana, Guadeloupe, Réunion, Martinique, French Polynesia, Mayotte, Wallis and Futuna, Saint-Pierre and Miquelon and New Caledonia.] ◆ Students will answer comprehension questions based on the reading, and add more information based on their prior knowledge. ◆ Instructor will present a vocabulary list of cognates. ◆ Students will define the words and categorize them by parts of speech (nouns, verbs, adjectives, etc.). Students will also find word associations to add to their vocabulary list such as adding the noun *antiracisme* to the existing vocabulary word *antiraciste*.

ANTIRACIST WORLD LANGUAGE LESSON TEMPLATE		
	Accessibilité *Antiraciste* *Classicisme* *Colonialisme* *Equité/Équitable* *Ethnique* *Ethnie* *Ethnicité* *Ethnocultural* *Exclusion* *Identité* *Immigrant* *Immigration* *Impérialisme* *Inclusion* *Intersectionnalité* *(une approche* *intersectionnelle)* *La ségrégation raciale* *La discrimination* *systémique*	*La diversité* *Les alliés* *Le genre* *La classe (la classe* *sociale)* *La ségrégation raciale* *L'oppression* *La marginalisation* *La diversité culturelle* *Le racisme* *La race* *Les préjugés* *La discrimination* *Le capitalisme* *L'identité racisée* *La justice raciale* *Raciale* *Racisé* *Systémique* *Un groupe ethnique*

	◆ **Viewing:** Students will watch two YouTube videos on race relations:
	   ◆ One video is the history of racism in France from the perspective of the French. This video is in French with no subtitles.
	   ◆ The other is an interview with Chimamanda Adichie, a Nigerian's perception of French racism. This video is in English.
	 ◆ **French video:** *Racisme en France: Le poids de l'histoire* (https://youtu.be/sh7x7HY6CbE).
	 ◆ **English interview** with Chimamanda Adichie (https://youtu.be/85zH4KDfJg4).
	 ◆ While viewing, students will take notes of the words and context that they hear in the videos or the words that are related to the video messaging.	

ANTIRACIST WORLD LANGUAGE LESSON TEMPLATE	
	Post-Viewing: ◆ Students will use the vocabulary to write their own paragraphs (5 sentences) describing what they learned from the video, what stood out to them. They can also incorporate responses to the essential questions. ◆ Students will meet in small groups to discuss their paragraphs. Each student must comment or ask a question of their peer. ◆ Following the small group discussions, one student from each group will present the main ideas from the various paragraphs to the whole class.
Assessments (Include summative or formative assessment delineated by communicative, interpretive and/or presentational modes.)	Student writings and discussions will serve as a summative assessment to determine their levels of comprehension of the video and responses to the essential questions.
Resources	**Additional Suggested Videos** Students can watch these additional videos to provide more context. *Histoire et évolution de l'empire colonial français* (https://youtu.be/yOWpL9iD4Xg) **Watch the following trailers or film clips that discuss French colonization:** *Rue cases-nègre* (https://youtu.be/fUM9ktYMDBw) *Salut Cousin* (https://youtu.be/N3m_b6kwIQY) *Camp de Thiaroye* (https://youtu.be/BOyD3u0vXvI)

References

American Council on the Teaching of Foreign Languages (ACTFL). (2015). *ACTFL performance descriptors for language learners.* www.actfl.org/resources/actfl-performance-descriptors-language-learners

Delpit, L. (2006). *Other people's children: Cultural conflict in the classroom.* The New Press.

Hawkins, M. (2017, March 19). Why not edit the text? *Maris Hawkins.* https://marishawkins.wordpress.com/2017/03/19/why-not-edit-the-text/

Ladson-Billings, G. (1995). Toward a theory of culturally relevant pedagogy. *American Educational Research Journal, 32*(3), 465–491.

Randolph, L.J. (2021, September 12). *Cultural and linguistic competence through social justice.* Webinar. Center for Educational Resources in Culture, Language and Literacy, University of Arizona. https://youtu.be/MgTWeV8Xl7c

Rubio, F. (2021, Spring). Program improvement, Part 2: Setting benchmarks and assessing proficiency. *The Language Educator, 16*(2), 16–19.

Rueckert, J. (2021, Spring). Evolving program benchmarks for higher levels of proficiency. *The Language Educator, 16*(2), 27–31.

Shrum, J.L., & Glisan, E.W. (2005). *Teacher's handbook: Contextualized language instruction* (3rd ed.). Thomson Heinle.

Shrum, J.L., & Glisan, E.W. (2010). *Teacher's handbook: Contextualized language instruction* (4th ed.). Thomson Heinle.

Wagner, M. (2021, May 26). *Teaching language for intercultural citizenship and social justice.* Webinar. Center for Educational Resources in Culture, Language and Literacy, University of Arizona. https://youtu.be/Ux5Lu0To-1s

8

Advocacy and Collaboration for the Antiracist World Language Classroom

"This book's framework is for *The Antiracist World Language Classroom*, but these principles could apply to all teachers across disciplines, educational leaders, Pre-K and beyond. Having a resource like this could help teachers to clearly articulate how they are meeting the standard of antiracism."
(Shana LeGrant, personal communication, October 14, 2021)

Two Pandemics: COVID-19 and Structural Racism

During 2020–2021, the nation was plagued with what many have termed *two pandemics*: COVID-19 and structural racism. We watched the world respond to the most pervasive global health crisis of the last century. We also witnessed communities across the globe rise up against police brutality both in the United States and abroad. Nations such as Hong Kong, Cuba, Brazil, Nigeria, Germany and many others stood with Black Lives Matter. How did these events impact the world language community?

DOI: 10.4324/9781003218265-9

Most world language organizations published statements condemning police brutality amid the deaths of George Floyd, Breonna Taylor, Ahmaud Arbery and countless others in the United States. Sadly, these atrocities did not stop at the U.S. border. Our global neighbors took note of the deaths of Adama Traoré in France and João Pedro Matos Pinto in Brazil, and the rising police violence in Nigeria, the United Kingdom and Hong Kong, to name but a few. Many language organizations also followed suit with resources and programming that centered anti-racism and social justice.

Language departments from early language to higher education offered professional development, workshops, conferences and keynotes on social justice and antiracism. ACTFL launched a web page titled Resources that Address Issues of Race, Diversity, and Social Justice. *The Language Educator* magazine's winter 2022 edition had a special focus topic titled Antiracism in the World Language Classroom. Regional language organizations heeded the call to address topics that had long been absent or dismissed from our discipline's discourse. In July 2021, the American Association of Teachers of Spanish and Portuguese (AATSP) dedicated an entire conference to diversity with the theme *Celebrando la diversidad: El español y el portugués; Celebrando a diversidade: O espanhol e o português.* The Southern Conference of Language Teachers (SCOLT) hosted a webinar titled, *Courageous Classrooms*, and there were so many other noteworthy responses. These programs have sparked national engagement on matters that have gone unvoiced and unnoticed by our mainstream professional organizations.

As a world language community, our sensitivities are heightened, we are continuing to skill build, and we are engaging in courageous conversations. What comes next? Though not an exhaustive list, the following are 10 actionable items that would take our journey to inclusion and representation to the next level (Glynn, Hines-Gaither, Jenkins, 2022).

10 ACTION STEPS TOWARD ANTIRACISM IN WORLD LANGUAGES

We need to…
1. Acknowledge and address what needs to change in our field such as bias, underrepresentation, microaggressions, racism and inequities.
2. Engage in strategic planning that allows for collective, broad-based action, sufficient time and resources to address underrepresentation.
3. Build alliances within languages and with other disciplines, organizations and affinity groups to expand our reach, pool our resources and to prioritize common goals.
4. Overtly name antiracism and social justice in existing language standards, guidelines and other framing documents. Draft antiracist and social justice standards that are specific to languages.
5. Articulate the return on investment and how languages benefit diverse communities of all proficiency levels.
6. Recruit and mentor diverse students and candidates into language programs, teacher education and professional organizations. Draft articulation agreements between departments and institutions to start early recruitment and to sustain ongoing pathways.
7. Review curriculum for bias and under/representation. Incorporate critical theories, antiracism, social justice, intersectionality, culturally responsive teaching and decolonization.
8. Revamp teacher education so that pre-service teachers leave their programs with the requisite dispositions, beliefs, advocacy and tools to support all learners.
9. Review world language policies and procedures at all levels (local to national) to determine how they help or hinder progress towards equity and representation.
10. Develop student, faculty and staff leaders in world languages who are equipped as advocates and agents of positive change.

Aligning Social Justice with Antiracism

Our profession is gaining ground on social justice, which is laudable. We seek to build on this momentum. For example, ACTFL has now published two editions of *Words and Actions: Teaching through the Lens of Social Justice* (Glynn et al., 2014, 2018). Most world language organizations have committed resources to social justice or diversity in the past few years. The Massachusetts Frameworks for World Languages now incorporates social justice as a key pillar. Few, however, have centered race, racism or antiracism. There is still discomfort with naming race and its enduring legacies. Yet, many of the languages we teach have direct connections to colonialism and imperialism. As we continue to highlight social justice and equity, antiracist teaching must be at the forefront of our endeavors.

In terms of **advocacy** for antiracism, we must create a world language platform that is race-focused. We cannot have an antiracist platform if we cannot acknowledge that race and racism exist and impact our field. The act of teaching a world language neither makes one social justice-minded nor antiracist. Antiracism and social justice are not equivalents. Someone can be passionate about social justice when it comes to certain issues such as gender, class or sexual orientation, but still ignore race altogether.

Shifting the Structure of Language Leadership

While many states have world language associations, they are not necessarily inclusive. A quick perusal of state and regional **language organizations** will quickly reveal how White the language profession is. For example, visit any state or regional language association website. Click on the Board of Directors tab. For those that have photos, take a look at the photos. How many people of color are shown? How many Black or African Americans are shown? How many Asians are depicted? How many Latinx or Indigenous people are there? As authors, we have done this. We find very few that have diverse representation in terms of race and ethnicity. We acknowledge that there may be invisible diversities within these boards that we cannot see such as religion, sexuality, disability, etc.; however, these invisible diversities should not give us a pass in seeking visible representation. Part of the issue is structural racism.

The 2021 SCOLT Teacher of the Year and Afro-Dominican, Jenniffer Whyte, observed:

> The first time that I attended a world language conference, I was surprised to see what I saw. In my mind, a world language conference is full of culture, colors, people from different countries, and possibly I thought I would see people dressed in typical cultural attire. To my surprise, the conference had no music from the target languages represented, no cultural attire, and the majority of the people were White. What happened to the people that look like me who teach Spanish or other languages? I was on a mission to find a workshop about African Americans or Afro-descendants. From hundreds of sessions listed, I found two. When I realized that these women of color were the only representation in the whole conference, I felt the need to do something about it. I thought, "where are the leaders?" Where are the people of color and why aren't they represented? I am a prime example of seeing a few leaders of color represented which propelled me to take action and support the cause.

Unfortunately, Jenniffer's observations are not unique. In preparing this book, we received too many stories relaying similar experiences. The fact that there are more White educators who major in world languages certainly impacts representation; however, there are thousands of BIPOC educators who systemically are not brought to the table. You want to know why? Representation has to be addressed at all levels (personal, interpersonal, cultural, institutional, systemic and curricular). On an institutional level, BIPOC language students are not mentored or encouraged to pursue higher levels of language study to the same degree as their White counterparts. Also, unlike their peers, language learners of color rarely have teachers who look like them or course content that reflects their identities. These factors, in turn, impact the number of students of color who major in languages. These outcomes also impact the representation in professional organizations. The state associations feed into the regional organizations. The regional organizations feed into the national ones.

If this issue is not addressed structurally, this dearth will persist. We must begin a fully **articulated** paradigm shift where anti-racism is centralized in all dimensions of the world language experience starting with the classroom itself and floating up the chain to the national organizations.

As long as the current structure is in place, our language profession will continue to be White-dominated. We recommend structural changes such as recruiting language educators from more diverse organizations to serve on national boards. For example, there are many language organizations that have large numbers of people of color. There is the College Language Association (CLA), composed predominantly of Black Educators of English and World Languages. ACTFL's Special Interest Group for Educators of African American Students (AAS SIG) draws standing room only crowds each year at the ACTFL convention. The AAS SIG supports both White and BIPOC educators who are committed to shifting the face of world languages.

Other diverse organizations include The Haitian Studies Association, the Caribbean Studies Association, the American Association of Teachers of Korean, the African Languages Teachers Association, the American Association of Teachers of French, American Association of Teachers of German, American Association of Teachers of Italian, the Association of Teachers of Japanese, the Chinese Language Teachers Association, the National Council of Less Commonly Taught Languages, the Latin American Studies Association, the Society for the Study of the Indigenous Languages of the Americas and a litany of others. Affinity groups in the world language profession abound such as African American Linguists (200+ members), Facebook groups like Black Spanish Teachers: ¿Qué tal? (300+ members), Incorporating Afro-Latino Culture in Spanish Classrooms (3,500 members) and the Native American and Indigenous Studies Association (9,600 members).

None of these organizations is in the pipeline or pathway to candidacies for local, regional or national language boards. If the structure shifted from solely pulling board members from traditionally supported state and regional language associations, there would be a more diverse pool from which to pull.

We recommend a certain number of ad hoc seats that would be dedicated to diverse associations or affinity groups.

Note, since diverse board members have traditionally not been at the table of most world language organizations, a serious internal climate audit will be needed to prepare for diverse membership. Attention will need to be given to implicit bias, microaggressions and the exclusive versus inclusive history of the organization. According to LePeau (2015), "The first step… is for … educators to consider the historical context and mission of the institution because this examination will offer greater insights about systems and institutional structures" (p. 183).

Teacher Education

Next, in terms of teacher education. We recommend that social justice and antiracism be foundational in the pre-service educator curriculum. Most teacher education programs give attention to diverse learners and how to support them. However, most of the mainstream methods textbooks do not include robust scholarship related to social justice or antiracism. Therefore, teacher candidates often leave their programs drastically underprepared to meet the needs and demands of a richly diverse student body. Even if the school is rather homogenous, all students need to gain the skills for engaging in a 21st century society that is likely far from homogenous.

We recommend partnerships between teacher education organizations and some of the affinity groups and diverse organizations aforementioned. Pre-service programs might also partner with historically Black colleges and universities, Hispanic-serving institutions, Indigenous-serving institutions, Asian American Pacific Islander-serving institutions and others. Partnerships might include offering training and in-service workshops to teacher education programs. We recommend that there be a serious assessment of teacher education methodology to include social justice and antiracism in meaningful ways.

Methodology textbooks should be supplemented with anti-racist scholarship. Disposition is typical in pre-service programs;

however, how is that measured for antiracism? We recommend that directors incorporate the *Six Dimensions of Antiracism in World Languages* as a framework for antiracist practice. Additionally, no teacher should enter the classroom without an understanding of the value added by home–school–community partnerships. Teachers must value their students, as well as their communities. "When teachers do not understand the potential of the students they teach, they will under teach them no matter what the methodology" (Delpit, 2006, p. 175).

Antiracist Collaborations for the Antiracist World Language Classroom

In 2019, James Tamm and Ronald Luyet wrote the book *Radical Collaboration: Five Essential Skills to Overcome Defensiveness and Build Successful Relationships*. Their book is related to managing conflicts and to working across differences. Building on the foundation of Tamm and Luyet, it is imperative that the world language profession also moves towards a model of radical collaboration.

Antiracist collaborations go beyond sharing lesson plans or professional learning communities. Radical collaborations are for and among individuals who make a commitment to antiracism. These individuals may span various levels of consciousness. They may be among language professionals or they may extend to students, families, communities and/or non-language professionals. One need not be an expert in antiracism to make a commitment to the foundational tenets. Anyone of any background can commit to radical collaborations. Christen Campbell, a White French teacher, entered a radical collaboration with Krishauna Hines-Gaither on centering the Black experience in Haiti and the Dominican Republic. They created a unit of study that focused on the two islands. Of the collaboration, Christen wrote:

> Without Krishauna's knowledge of the Dominican culture, I believe my research would have been incomplete… Furthermore, and perhaps more importantly, our collaboration acted as a model for peace between two divided cultures.

> There was no rivalry of which country, language or culture was more important; rather a seamless unity of diversity.
>
> (C. Campbell, personal communication, October 1, 2019)

This collaboration exemplifies that what the two educators created together was far more powerful than what either could have created alone. It is time for the language community to step outside of itself. We need to look to colleagues in other disciplines to gain new tools. We need to start conversations with those who impact our profession such as guidance counselors and Advanced Placement coordinators.

Haitian Kreyòl and French professor, Lovia Mondésir noted:

> One essential element is to teach minority students that they belong in language classes, that knowing a language is not a White privilege. Learning a language can have an equalizing effect, and open doors to different worlds that minoritized students may not have access to or even know exist.
>
> (personal communication, July 20, 2021)

Oftentimes guidance counselors may not have a full understanding of how languages work, and they may have biases on who should or should not pursue language courses. The language educator should engage with these colleagues so that they are on one accord.

Your students should also be your collaborators. They enter the classroom with a social foundation. They have navigated their lives from their unique positionalities. Your students have access to communities that you may not. As a non-native Spanish professor, Krishauna has always appreciated the insights and contributions of her native speaker students. Recently, when preparing to give a keynote address to AATSP, Krishauna wanted to incorporate Portuguese into her discourse. She called upon one of her students Milene Ferreira Henriques from Portugal to assist her. Milene, in turn, connected Krishauna with her mother, whom she felt was more well versed in the language. The mom verified Krishauna's pronunciation and explained to her the different sentence structures and vocabularies between speakers of Portuguese from Portugal versus Brazil. This collaboration made the speech richer and more authentic.

As the instructor, intentionally cultivate a spirit of collaboration with your students. What the collaboration entails will depend upon factors such as your classroom structure, the number of students, the modality (face to face, online, hybrid), etc. The instructor has the power to set the collaborative tone. In so doing, be mindful that some students from dominant groups (in terms of their racial/ethnic, gender, sexual identities, abilities, etc.) do not take up more social and physical space than others. Wolof teacher Marie Correa-Fernandes stated: "[w]hen in the presence of minority or marginalized groups in my classroom, I make sure to engage every student in the activities so that no-one feels left out" (personal communication, July 8, 2021). Educators should create the paradigm that represents the collaborative model that they would like to see in the classroom.

Modeling antiracist collaboration serves as a microcosm for positive interaction across differences, even beyond the classroom. In the language community, there needs to be an infusion of radical love. Harlem Renaissance writer and racial justice advocate James Baldwin stated: "If I love you, I have to make you conscious of the things you don't see." The work of antiracism is too important for egos. We have to be able to admit what we do not know, where we have failed and where we need help. We have to remain humble enough to receive support. Conversely, we must not become social justice or antiracist elitists who possess an air of superiority and condescension. No matter how far we may or may not be on our journey, there is always growth that lies ahead.

Following are tenets that guide antiracist collaborations:

Tenets for Antiracist Collaborations
1. Name your why. Articulate why antiracism is essential to the world language classroom. What is your philosophy of antiracism?
2. Own what you do not know. Do your work by studying, engaging and showing up in spaces where antiracist praxis is being disseminated.

Tenets for Antiracist Collaborations
3. Spend time cultivating authentic relationships with world language professionals who can fill gaps in knowledge. Also, cultivate relationships beyond world language professionals in other disciplines and spheres of influence.
4. Engage in the communities that you serve. Beyond the classroom, get to know the environments of your students.
5. Audit your course content to ensure that multiple perspectives that include antiracist practices are centered.
6. Engage in radical sharing. Develop a mechanism to share antiracist content with colleagues to build an antiracist portal of information and content.
7. Make antiracism highly visible. Ask yourself this fundamental question: *How will your students, colleagues and the community know that you are committed to antiracism?*

Ask Yourself!

◆ How have you engaged in antiracist collaborations in your classroom, school, department or in the field as a whole?

Shana LeGrant, consultant with the University of North Carolina Frank Porter Graham Child Development Institute, shared that "districts are craving antiracism and culturally responsive teaching. We have the *what*, but we lack the *how*. School leaders at all levels are engaging in this discussion, and see the need to sharpen their antiracism skills." Bearing these sentiments in mind, we now focus on how school leaders can support the critical work of antiracism.

We asked language colleagues from across the country how school leaders could best support the work of antiracism. Some of their suggestions follow.

"Leaders should directly ask language teachers about their antiracist work. It should be part of our daily practice, evaluation, meetings, and expectations."
Adriana Ramírez, Spanish, Semiahmoo Secondary School

"Leaders need to first educate themselves on the tenets of White supremacy and culture. Then they should identify how this culture manifests itself at their school. Leaders should listen to BIPOC staff without asking them to speak for everyone else. Leaders should support long-term work instead of seeking quick fixes."
Cécile Lainé, French, Toward Proficiency

"Leaders need to work together with the teachers, students and the government to change educational policies that best support antiracist programs."
Anne Francois-Hurley, French, Arcadia University

"Leaders must provide funding for quality training and instructional resources selected by the world language educators themselves. For efficacy, it must be a bottom-up, not top-down approach."
Michelle Fulwider-Westall, Spanish, World Language Instructional Designer

"Leaders should hire outside consultants to engage in professional development. Recognize the inequities that are facing our communities and share them with the larger school community. I think sometimes administrators are fearful of not being on the same page as their constituents, and it is true, being an administrator is very much about being neutral; however, when it comes to racism, being silent is being complicit."
Christen Campbell, French, Chapel Hill High School

"Leaders can support antiracism by increasing the diversity in students and faculty." *Marie Correa-Fernandes, Wolof, University of Kansas*

How Leaders can Support Antiracist World Language Programs	
District Level	◆ Verbalize your district's support for and commitment to antiracism. ◆ Align district standard course of study with the ACTFL *World Readiness Standards, Proficiency Guidelines* and *Can-Do Statements*. ◆ Expand the above-mentioned framing documents to include antiracism in your district (see www.doe.mass.edu/frameworks/world-languages/2021.pdf, page 11). ◆ Challenge textbook companies to ensure that textbooks have an antiracism component. ◆ Adopt companion texts such as *The Antiracist World Language Classroom, Words and Actions: Teaching through the Lens of Social Justice* (Glynn et al., 2018) and others. ◆ Offer antiracist professional development to the entire district of world language educators. ◆ Offer a range of professional development that is both broad, to reach multiple disciplines, and also specific to world languages. ◆ Invest in external consultants to assess the district's antiracist practices, and to offer ongoing professional development. ◆ Review and address district policies that promote racist practices and inequitable outcomes. ◆ Consider how antiracism goals support larger district initiatives such as graduation rates, higher enrolment in AP classes, etc. ◆ Understand that there may be pushback from parents, students, teachers and community members due to the inclusion of antiracism. Establish how you will support antiracism within your district.

How Leaders can Support Antiracist World Language Programs	
Principals	◆ Verbalize support for and commitment to antiracism for your school. Review https://tinyurl.com/52ed4uj5 ◆ Study, support and promote the elements of cultural proficiency for principals from National Association of Elementary School Principals or use similar frameworks: https://tinyurl.com/4h6e7f47 ◆ Study, support and promote how to be an antiracist leader using work such as that of Dena Simmons: https://tinyurl.com/2va7wyxk ◆ Support ongoing antiracist professional development at your school. ◆ Encourage teachers to represent your school at district level meetings on the topic of antiracism and other related topics such as school equity. ◆ Invite BIPOCs to the table related to antiracism/equity discussions, but also expand the pool to White colleagues to hear different perspectives and to avoid burnout and abuse of BIPOC faculty. ◆ Review and address school policies that promote anti/racist practices and in/equitable outcomes. ◆ Have accountability measures in place to ensure antiracist classrooms are operating optimally, and to encourage antiracist practices and dispositions. ◆ Since most language teachers will have to supplement antiracist teaching materials, offer a budget for the purchase of supplemental materials (including books such as Glynn et al., 2018), etc. ◆ Provide funding and support for non-print materials such as podcasts, YouTube videos, films, electronic magazine/journal subscriptions, etc. ◆ Expand your list of school partners to include BIPOC communities. ◆ Organize a community advisory board that is composed of parents/families, community members and stakeholders who can bring diverse perspectives to your school. ◆ Invest in external consultants to assess the school's antiracist practices, and to offer ongoing professional development. ◆ Understand that there may be pushback from parents, students, teachers and community members due to the inclusion of antiracism. Establish how you will support antiracism within your school. ◆ Consider how antiracism goals support larger school initiatives such as the school mission, anti-bullying, etc.

How Leaders can Support Antiracist World Language Programs	
Department Chairs	◆ For your department, verbalize support for and commitment to antiracism. ◆ Have common departmental goals for antiracism. ◆ Develop antiracist skills and capacity as a team through engagement in regular professional learning communities. ◆ Coordinate on antiracist units of study and daily lessons within the language department. ◆ Coordinate on antiracist units of study and daily lessons across disciplines and departments. ◆ Invest in antiracist departmental speakers who can add value to the department. ◆ Collaborate with other departments to invite antiracist speakers to the school. ◆ Have accountability measures within your department to encourage antiracist practices and dispositions. ◆ Ensure that antiracism is evenly integrated into the world language program, and not just during celebratory months such as Native American Heritage Month, Hispanic/Latinx Heritage Month, Black History Month, Asian Heritage Month, etc. ◆ Review and address departmental policies that promote anti/racist practices and in/equitable outcomes. ◆ Organize a community advisory board that is composed of parents/families, community members and stakeholders who can bring diverse perspectives to your program. ◆ Understand that there may be pushback from parents, students, teachers and community members due to the inclusion of antiracism. Establish how you will support antiracism within your department. ◆ Partner with university language programs to offer support for your K-12 antiracist programs. ◆ Serve on policy-driven committees within your district, state, region or nationally to promote antiracism. ◆ Have a mechanism for hearing from students, teachers and communities on antiracism needs. ◆ Consider how antiracism goals support larger departmental initiatives such as increased enrollment in higher level courses, etc. ◆ Respect the expertise that already exists on the topic of antiracism within your department.
Guidance Counselors	◆ Be knowledgeable about the role guidance counselors play in placing students in classrooms and courses. ◆ Work from a paradigm of "all learners are capable" as opposed to deficit-based approaches. ◆ Where possible, ensure there is a diverse mix of students in world language classrooms, and not only one BIPOC in a section.

How Leaders can Support Antiracist World Language Programs	
	◆ Work with teachers to encourage students of color to enroll in Advanced Placement classes and to take the accompanying exam. ◆ Make sure students' unique identities are represented and celebrated. ◆ Work to reduce the perception of BIPOC students who enroll in honors classes as either not belonging there, or as acting White. ◆ Encourage students of color to pursue language study beyond the minimum district requirement. ◆ Be aware of and promote the myriad of opportunities for students of color to study languages, to study abroad and to receive financial assistance such as: https://clscholarship.org/ or https://weboaal.com/scholarship ◆ Work in collaboration with world language departments to learn from them how you can best support their antiracist programs. ◆ Align language and antiracism goals with college, career and job readiness. ◆ Partner with university language programs to gain insights into what students need to know when applying to college language programs. ◆ Consider how antiracism goals support larger school initiatives such as increased graduation rates, college acceptance rates, etc.
Professional Organizations	◆ Review policies that may serve to hinder diversity, equity and inclusion. For example, do you allow job postings within your organizations that will reach diverse candidates? ◆ Restructure your boards. Ensure that you are providing outreach and opportunities to diverse pools of language educators. ◆ Work closely with organizations, associations and affinity groups that have the diversity that you seek. ◆ So that your organization is prepared to receive BIPOC board members, do internal work such as anti-bias and microaggressions training. ◆ Create ad-hoc board positions that ensure that BIPOC individuals have a seat at the table. ◆ Review conference programs so that there is ample representation of BIPOC presenters who engage antiracism in their presentations. Ensure that their time slots and room locations are fair and equitable.

References

Delpit, L. (2006). *Other people's children: Cultural conflict in the classroom*. The New Press.

Glynn, C., Wesely, P., & Wassell, B. (2014). *Words and actions: Teaching languages through the lens of social justice*. American Council on the Teaching of Foreign Languages.

Glynn, C., Wesely, P., & Wassell, B. (2018). *Words and actions: Teaching languages through the lens of social justice* (2nd ed.). American Council on the Teaching of Foreign Languages.

Glynn, C., Hines-Gaither, K., & Jenkins, T. (2022). Increasing black representation in languages: Lessons from the past and present. *The Language Educator*.

LePeau, L.A. (2015). The transformational potential of academic affairs and student affairs partnerships for enacting multicultural initiatives. In S. Watt (Ed.), *Designing transformational multicultural initiatives: Theoretical foundations, practical applications, and facilitator considerations* (pp. 180–190). Stylus Publishing.

Tamm, J.W. & Luyet, R.J. (2019). *Radical collaboration: Five essential skills to overcome defensiveness and build successful relationships* (2nd ed.). Harper Business.